So! I'M A NEW **GRAPHIC DESIGNER** WHAT'S NEXT?

Carole Maugé-Lewis, MFA

Linda L. McCulloch, contributing author, Chapter FOUR (Special Section), "What Job is Right For Me?" brings her unique insights on "Choosing the right work environment."

Cover design by the Maugé-Lewis.

ISBN: 979-8-9904141-2-9

For corrections, inquiries about interviews or speaking engagements, please contact
mymaugedesign@gmail.com

DEDICATION

This book is dedicated to aspiring graphic design students, the home-schooled, career changers, self-taught designers, entry-level designers, Art and Design students, creative entrepreneurs, design enthusiasts, and especially to educators and instructors, who want additional resources to guide their students in graphic design studies.

ACKNOWLEDGMENTS

I express my gratitude to The Almighty for guidance and blessings received throughout the process of creating this book, my second publication in my field of expertise, graphic design.

Thank you to everyone who has played a role in bringing this book to fruition. Your contributions have made a significant impact. I am truly appreciative.

Special Section by Contributing Author, Linda L. McCulloch:
Sincere thanks to Linda for her addition to CHAPTER FOUR (Special Section), "What Job is Right For Me?" bringing her unique insights on "Choosing the right work environment." Her professional input is a welcome addition to this title.

Linda L. McCulloch is a graduate of the Ringling College of Art and Design, and Owner of *Design That Works*, an award-winning graphic design and marketing communications company (since 1987).

Linda McCulloch gratefully acknowledges Carole Maugé-Lewis for inviting me along on this journey; also my sincere thanks to the designers who contributed to the "What Real World Designers Say" in my special section: ***Lindsay Muncy, Alaina Voerg, Jill Carson*** and ***Janie Morgan.*** I am also eternally grateful for my loving, wonderful, equally talented husband, Michael, and his never-ending encouragment to me along with his belief that no matter how badly I may feel, I am still "magnificent." And to our house panther Milo, who "assisted" my writing by sitting on my lap so I could only work with one hand.

Last but not least, my profound thanks to Hilary Price, one of my favorite cartoonists of all time, who graciously allowed us to use six of her earlier strips relating to graphic designers in our book, for a reasonable fee. Hilary B. Price is an American cartoonist, known for creating the comic strip *Rhymes with Orange,* which is published digitally on her website and in over one hundred newspapers across the United States. At the age of 25 she became the youngest cartoonist to ever be nationally syndicated. She won the Silver Reuben for "Best Newspaper Panel Cartoon" from the National Cartoonists Society four times, in 2006, 2009, 2012, and 2014; was nominated for the 2013 Reuben Award, and won the InkPot Award in 2015, annually awarded at Comic-Con in San Diego, California.

Editor:
Cherie K. Miller has an MA in Professional Writing and an MA Certificate in American Studies from Kennesaw State University. She was an educational professional for almost 20 years, serving in the Coles College of Business and the Radow College of Humanities. She has written or co-written four books and has over 200 published articles in magazines. Cherie is passionate about reading and the written word. She was thrilled to contribute to this series!

For the unwavering support of my son Kevin, who has always stood by me and been enthusiastic about my journey as an author. Many thanks.

Carole

AN OVERVIEW OF THE AUTHOR'S CAREER, FROM BEING A STUDENT TO BECOMING A GRAPHIC DESIGNER TO EVENTUALLY BECOMING AN EDUCATOR

Carole's career began when she was an undergraduate student studying Art at Howard University in Washington, D.C. She pursued a major in graphic design after switching from her original Painting major. Carole's talent and dedication were recognized, and she became the first ever undergraduate teaching assistant in the Department of Art in the College of Fine Arts. She later served as the graduate teaching assistant.

Carole's skills as a freelance designer quickly gained recognition. She became the go-to student designer for clients seeking graphic design projects from the department. Eventually, she became the exclusive designer for gallery publications within the department. Carole created visually stunning posters and programs for faculty exhibits, as well as exhibitions featuring international artists. Her expertise in using bold dynamic typography to visually narrate stories was evident in her poster designs and is still evident in her book cover designs today.

As an undergraduate student, Carole gained practical experience in newspaper design at the Columbia Flyer, in Maryland, and at a traditional printshop in the area, where she developed a deep understanding of prepress and the printing process. Additionally, she had the fortune of interning at the Smithsonian, where she further honed her typography skills, working on labels and signage for artifact displays under the guidance of a mentor from the institution. Simultaneously, Carole continued to learn, practice, and contribute to various museum projects. After completing her Bachelor of Fine Arts degree in Graphic Design, Carole secured a position as the Visual Information Specialist at the Department of Consumer and Regulatory Affairs in Washington, D.C. She spent a year in this role before returning to Howard University to pursue a master's degree in graphic design.

Carole's educational journey started while she was an undergraduate student. She had the privilege of learning from outstanding professors and being assigned challenging and meaningful projects. Students actively participated in constructive critiques to improve their work. Carole excelled in this environment, creating her best work, and realizing her potential for personal growth. During her time as both an undergraduate and graduate teaching assistant, Carole gained invaluable experience. After earning her Master of Fine Arts degree in graphic design, she was offered a position as an Assistant Professor in the department where she eagerly shared her knowledge, and developed a deep passion for teaching design and nurturing young minds for the future. This marked the beginning of her career as an educator.

In 1995, Carole was recruited by Kennesaw State University to establish their graphic design program. Working closely with the department chair, she spearheaded the setup of the only computer lab equipped with a few Macintosh computers, eventually assisting the entire Art department in transitioning from PC to Mac. Carole also authored the print-focused courses for the graphic design program and introduced students to HTML and website design as the demand for designers with those skills grew. Although Carole primarily considered herself a print designer, she advocated for the hiring of additional faculty members specializing in web design, and other digitally-focused courses, most now being offered in the School of Art and Design (SOAAD).

Carole has skillfully balanced teaching fundamental design skills with adapting to the rapidly changing world of media, technology, and culture. Under her guidance, her students have achieved remarkable success, winning awards at both local and international levels. Many of her past students now excel in roles such as Art Directors, Brand Managers, Web Designers, and Marketing Specialists in the graphic design industry. Some have even built impressive careers at renowned companies like Disney, Facebook, and Apple, while a few have pursued entrepreneurship by starting their own design businesses.

Carole remains dedicated to her passion for teaching, designing, and writing about graphic design. Carole is presently the owner of an award-winning book cover design business, maugedesign.online.

MILTON GLASER FAMOUSLY STATED:

"There are three responses to a piece of design – yes, no, and WOW! Wow is the one to aim for."

TABLE OF CONTENTS

TABLE OF CONTENTS

INTRODUCTION

Each chapter in this book provides practical insights, actionable advice, and real-world examples to guide aspiring designers on their journey to securing their first job and launching a fulfilling career in graphic design. From refining portfolios and resumes to cultivating a professional online presence, communicating with clients, and mastering the art of networking, this book is an invaluable resource and guide. Chapter Four, titled "Navigating the Job Market," offers a special section by contributing author, Linda L. McCulloch, with a detailed overview and expert guidance on deciding on the right environment, whether it be Corporate In-House, Institutional In-House, Design Firm, Marketing/Advertising Agency, or Freelance. Whether you're a recent graduate eager to land a dream job or a seasoned professional looking to stay ahead of the curve, this book will help you navigate the challenges and opportunities in the ever-evolving world of graphic design.

For graduating senior designers, having an updated portfolio is essential. It serves as a powerful tool to showcase their latest and best work, highlighting their skills, and distinguishing themselves in the job market. Creating a comprehensive and polished portfolio greatly improves career prospects in the graphic design industry.

Even for designers without much formal education, using mockups of self-initiated projects is an excellent strategy to create a strong portfolio. The focus should be similar to those with formal design education. By emphasizing high-quality mockups, documenting the process, and presenting work professionally, a compelling portfolio can be created that effectively showcases skills and potential, even without extensive formal education.

In addition, designers should consider obtaining reference letters from professors, mentors, or even from volunteer work. While a strong portfolio and resume are essential for a job application, receiving positive recommendations from trusted mentors and educators can greatly enhance a candidate's credibility and appeal to potential employers. Whether a graduating senior seeking a first job, a freelancer, or a seasoned professional looking to advance a career, utilizing reference letters can be a game-changer in the pursuit of success in the field of graphic design. Reference letters can help graduating seniors and designers in general to distinguish themselves in a competitive job market and make a lasting impression on hiring managers.

Throughout this book, we provide valuable insights into the process of continuing professional growth and education. Additionally, we explore the concept of making a lasting impact and discuss how it can lead to a successful career change.

CHAPTER ONE

PREPARING FOR THE JOURNEY AHEAD

Preparation for the Journey Ahead

This chapter delves into the transition from student to professional, covering essential steps such as preparing or updating your portfolio, fine-tuning your resume, and networking strategies to secure job opportunities. Evaluating your portfolio is essential to being able to update and refine it effectively.

Tips for selecting diverse pieces that highlight your skills and versatility:

Evaluate Your Current Portfolio:

Begin by reviewing your existing portfolio to determine its strengths and areas for improvement. Take note of any outdated or weaker pieces that may need to be removed or updated. Consider your goals and target audience when selecting the content for your portfolio. For instance, if you want to highlight your layout and typography skills, avoid overwhelming your portfolio with illustrations. Instead, you can incorporate your illustrations into a page layout along with headlines and body text to showcase your diverse skill set and typographic skills.

Keep in mind that your portfolio should always be tailored to the specific types of jobs you are applying for. As each job opportunity may require different skills, updating and refining your portfolio should be an ongoing process. **And, if you do not have a portfolio begin assembling one now!**

Follow these steps to evaluate your portfolio:

1. Define Your Audience and Review Goals: Consider your career goals, target audience, and the purpose of your portfolio. Align your portfolio with your goals and cater to your intended audience's needs and expectations.

2. Select Your Best Work and Assess Content Quality: Evaluate the quality of your portfolio's work. Consider factors like creativity, technical skill, innovation, and relevance to your target audience. Remove pieces that no longer represent your current skill level or style, and that don't align with your goals. Focus on quality over quantity and showcase a diverse range of projects that highlight your skills, expertise, and versatility as a designer.

4. Organize Your Portfolio: Determine the best way to organize your portfolio to effectively showcase your work. You may organize your projects chronologically, by type of work (e.g., branding, print design, web design), or by client or industry. Ensure that your portfolio is easy to navigate and presents your work in a cohesive and engaging manner. Check for consistency in style, theme, and presentation. Ensure all pieces work together to create a cohesive visual narrative.

5. Update Project Descriptions: Provide clear and concise descriptions for each project in your portfolio. Highlight the objectives, challenges, and outcomes of each project, along with your role and contributions. Use storytelling to engage the viewer and provide context for your work. Make sure to proofread and spellcheck all copy.

6. Include Case Studies or Process Documentation: Consider including case studies or process documentation for select projects in your portfolio. This allows you to provide deeper insights into your design process, problem-solving skills, and thought processes, which can be valuable for potential clients or employers, especially if you're not present when the portfolio is being reviewed.

7. Include Visuals and Examples: Supplement your case studies with visuals, such as sketches, wireframes, prototypes, or mockups, to illustrate key points and provide concrete examples of your work in action.

8. Highlight Your Role and Contributions: If part of a team, clearly state your role in each project and outline your specific contributions. This helps demonstrate your expertise and level of involvement in the project's success. It also reflects your teamsmanship.

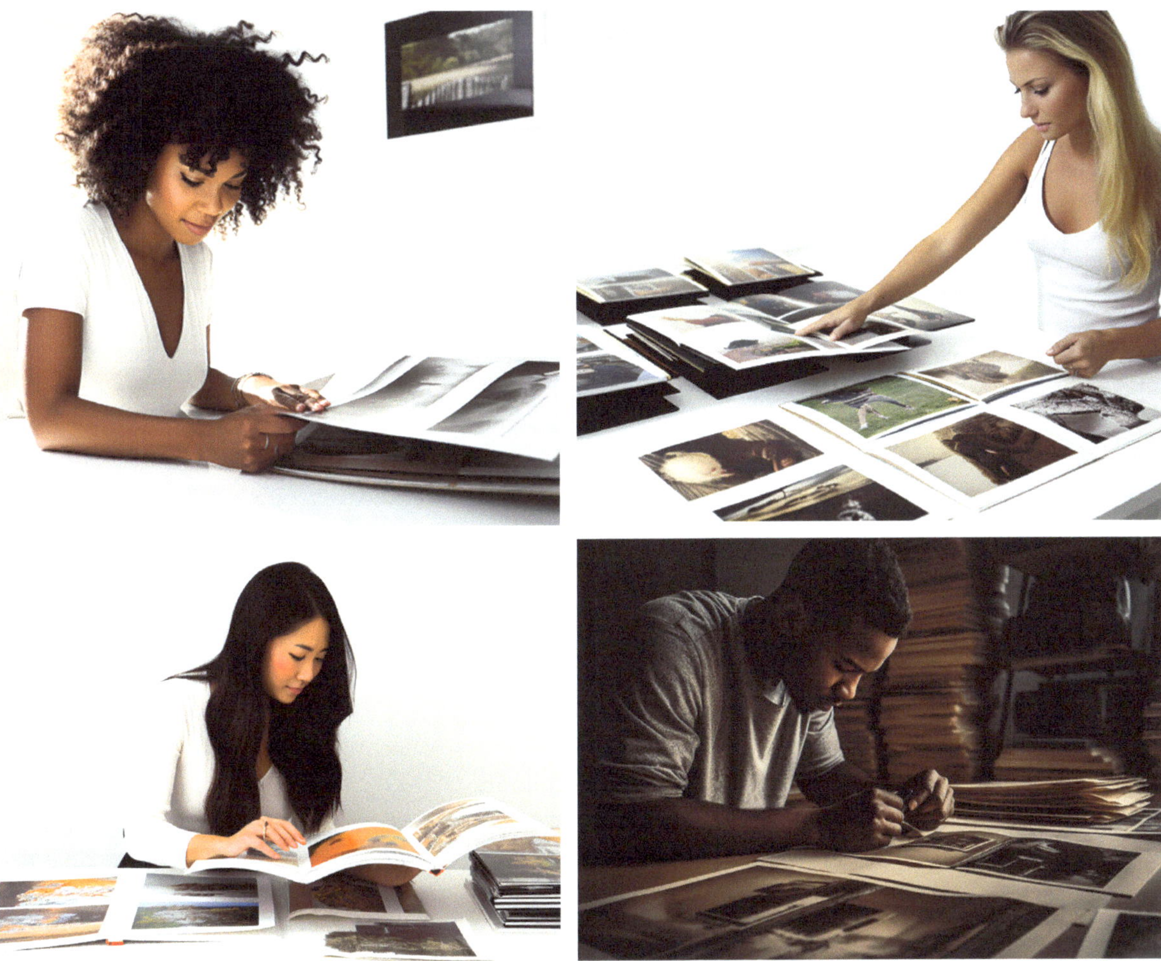

Designers preparing for the journey ahead, by carefully assessing and updating their portfolio to present their best work.

9. Evaluate Presentation: Assess the overall presentation and organization of your portfolio. Is it easy to navigate, visually appealing, and engaging? Pay attention to layout, typography, image quality, and user experience. Enhance the visual appeal and usability of your portfolio to be memorable. Tailor your portfolio to highlight projects that align with your audience's needs and interests.

10. Update Your Online Presence: If you have an online portfolio, make sure it is up to date and reflects your latest work and achievements. It should also be easy to navigate and user-friendly. Besides keeping your portfolio current, prioritize optimizing it for mobile devices. Since more people are using mobile devices to browse the Internet, it is crucial that your portfolio website is responsive and provides a seamless experience on different screen sizes.

Evaluate the navigation of your website and ensure it is intuitive and easy to use. Visitors should be able to find the information they're looking for, such as your portfolio pieces, contact information, and about page, without any trouble.

Maintain consistency in branding across all your online platforms, including your portfolio website and any social media profiles. Highlight your most recent work and achievements prominently on your portfolio website. You may want to feature recent projects on the homepage or create a dedicated section to showcase your recent accomplishments. This will reinforce your professional identity and provide a cohesive experience for visitors.

11. Seek Feedback: Gather feedback from peers, mentors, or industry professionals. Solicit constructive criticism and suggestions for improvement. Incorporate feedback to refine and strengthen your portfolio.

Choose reviewers who can provide valuable insights based on their expertise and experience in the design industry. This could include peers, mentors, professors, or professionals in your desired field.

When seeking feedback, be specific about what aspects of your portfolio you would like reviewers to focus on. For example, you might ask for feedback on the clarity of your project descriptions, the effectiveness of your visual presentation, or the overall user experience of your website.

Seek feedback from trusted individuals with diverse perspectives and backgrounds. This can help you gather a range of opinions and identify areas for improvement that you may not have considered on your own.

Approach feedback with an open mind and a willingness to accept constructive criticism. Remember that the goal is to improve your portfolio and enhance its effectiveness in showcasing your skills and accomplishments.

12. Regularly Maintain and Update: Keep your portfolio fresh and up to date by regularly adding new work and removing outdated or weaker pieces. Keep the sleeves of the portfolio clean or replace them with new ones. Set aside time periodically to review and update your portfolio to ensure that it continues to showcase your best work effectively.

Establish a schedule to regularly review and update your portfolio. You can choose to do this quarterly, biannually, or annually depending on your preferences and career goals. When adding new work to your portfolio, make sure that it meets the same high standards as your existing pieces. Be selective about which projects you include. Stay updated on industry trends, technological advancements, and changes in design standards. Incorporate relevant updates into your portfolio to demonstrate your adaptability and relevance in the field.

Encourage interaction with your online portfolio by including features such as a blog, newsletter, or social media integration. This will allow you to share updates, insights, and behind-the-scenes content with your audience, keeping them engaged and informed about your latest work and activities.

By following these steps, you can evaluate your portfolio effectively and identify areas for improvement. This will help ensure that your portfolio always showcases your best work and helps you achieve your career goals, even when you're not present for its review. Your portfolio should speak for itself, especially in your absence.

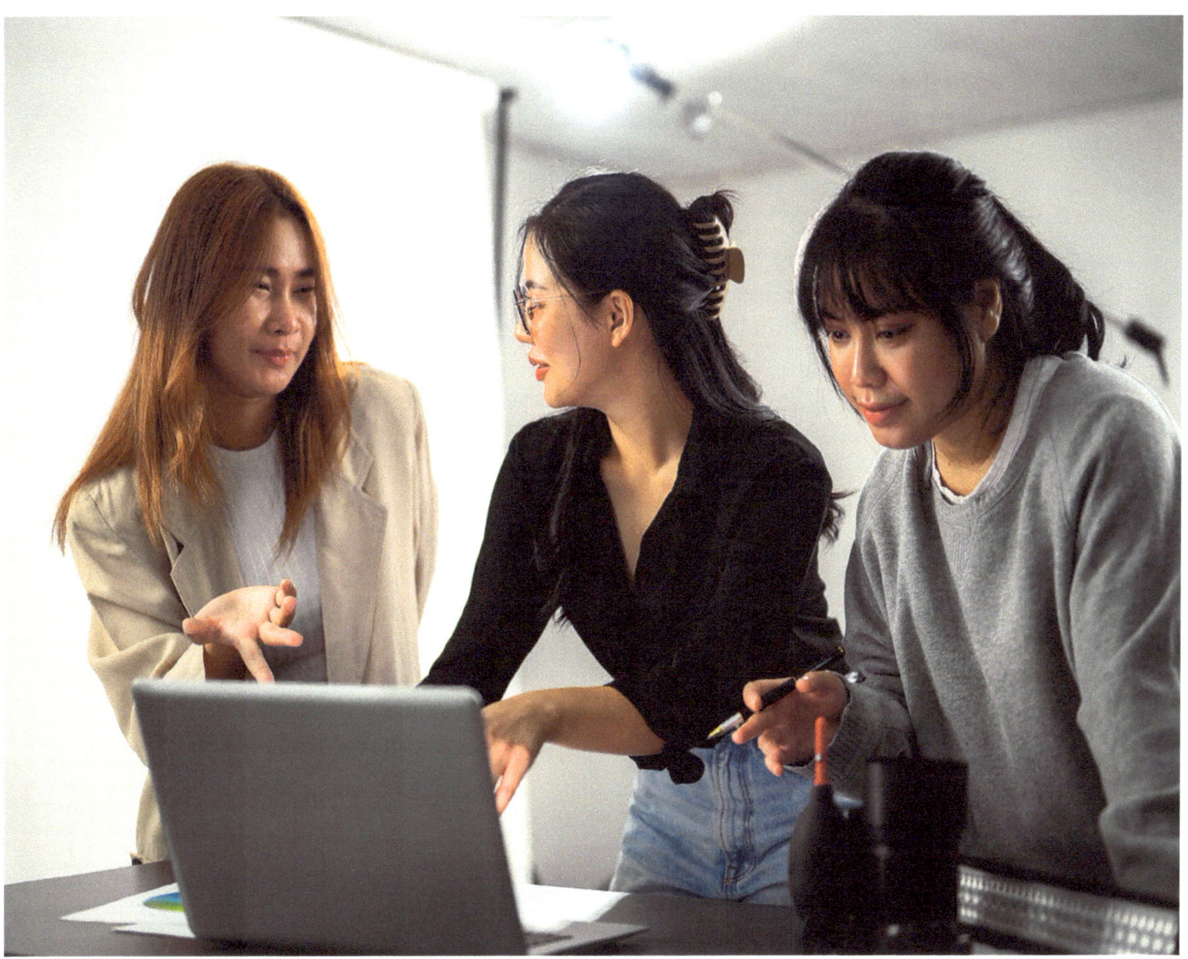

Designer sharing and reviewing work to solicit constructive criticism and suggestions from peers for refinement to strengthen their portfolio.

Choosing a Portfolio Style

Graphic designers have a variety of portfolio sizes and style options to choose from to present their body of graphic design work, from traditional to hybrid.

Here are some common styles:

1. Traditional Print Portfolio: This is a physical portfolio that includes printed samples of your best work. It is usually presented in a professional binder or portfolio case. This format allows for hands-on interaction with your designs and is ideal for in-person meetings or interviews.

2. Digital Portfolio Website: An online portfolio website that showcases your work in a digital format. It provides easy access to your portfolio from anywhere with an internet connection and allows for customization, interactivity, and multimedia elements like videos or animations.

3. PDF Portfolio: A digital portfolio compiled into a PDF document that can be easily shared via email or downloaded from a website. This format offers flexibility in design and layout and is suitable for sending to potential clients or employers as an attachment.

4. Presentation Portfolio: A dynamic presentation format where you showcase your work using presentation software like PowerPoint, Keynote, Prezi, Adobe Spark Ludus, and Visme among others. Each of these tools offers unique features that can enhance your presentation and make it stand out, depending on your specific needs and preferences.

5. Social Media Portfolio: Sharing your work on social media platforms such as Instagram, Behance, or Dribbble. This format facilitates easy sharing, networking, and engagement with a wider audience of fellow designers, potential clients, and industry professionals.

6. Interactive Portfolio: A multimedia portfolio that incorporates interactive elements like clickable links, scroll effects, sliders, or interactive prototypes. This format provides a more immersive and engaging experience for viewers, highlighting your design skills in action. This can also be done with an Interactive PDF, or online intuitive website builders like Squarespace and Wix among others.

7. Case Study Portfolio: A portfolio that includes detailed case studies of your projects, offering insights into your design process, problem-solving approach, and outcomes. This format allows you to demonstrate your expertise, strategic thinking, and results-oriented design approach.

8. Hybrid Portfolio: A combination of different portfolio formats tailored to your specific needs and preferences. For example, you might have a digital portfolio website as your primary showcase and complement it with a printed portfolio for in-person meetings or presentations.

Ultimately, the choice of portfolio style depends on factors such as your target audience, career goals, personal preferences, and the type of work you want to showcase. It is important to select a format that effectively showcases your skills, experience, and personality as a designer while meeting the needs and expectations of your intended audience.

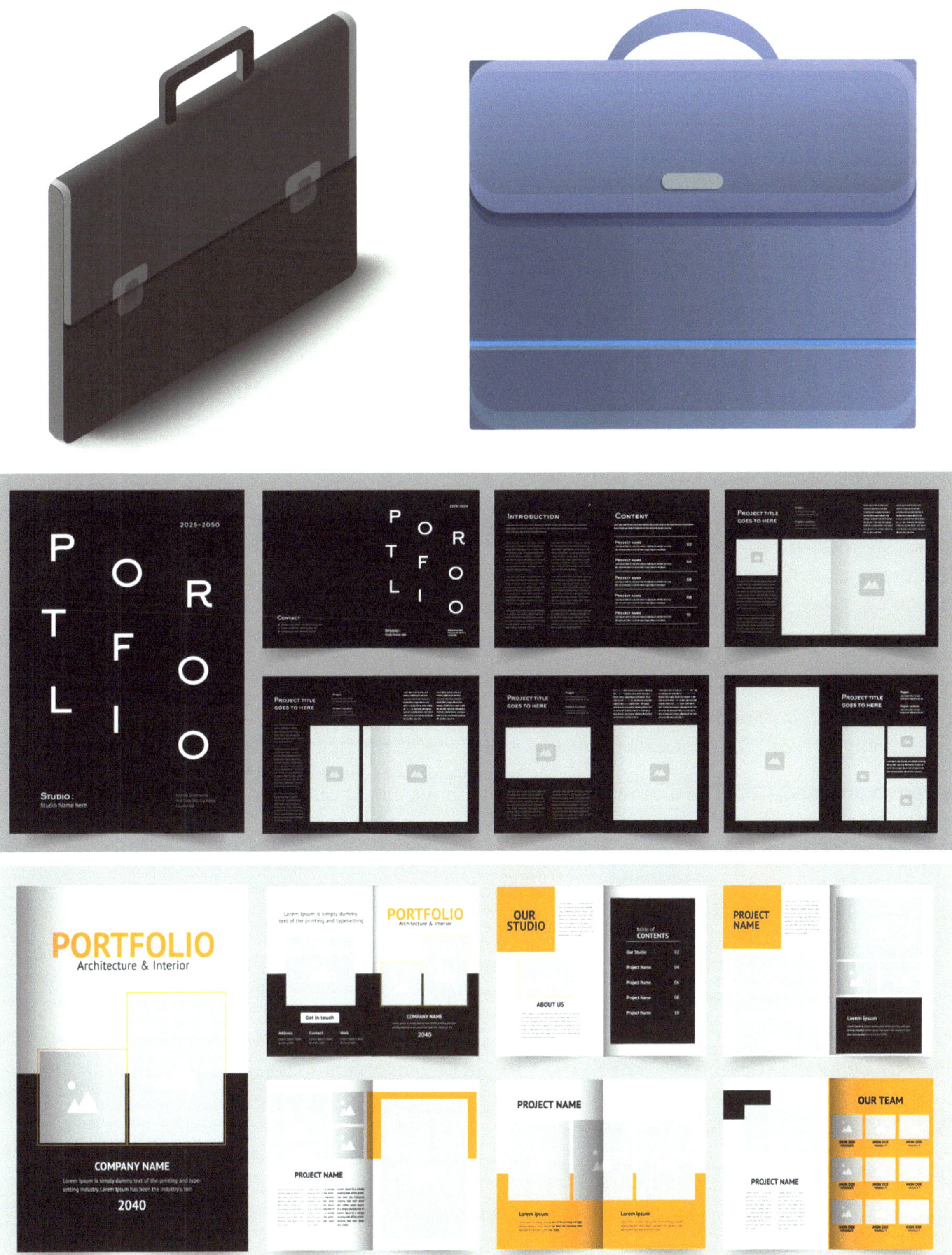

Above: *Different color and styles of portfolios should reflect your personal syle and brand, and the type of work you are showcasing.*

Below: *Two portfolios opened to show detailed case studies of projects, offering insights into the designer's process, problem-solving approaches, and outcomes. Both formats allow you to demonstrate your expertise, strategic thinking, layout skills and results-oriented design approach.*

Does the color and design of my portfolio matter?

Portfolios do not always need to be black, as was traditional thinking. Sometime a small accent color can spark interest and have visual impact. Ultimately, the choice of color and design for your portfolio should serve to enhance your work and make a positive impression on viewers, and is well-organized, visually cohesive, and professional.

Here are some factors to consider when deciding on the color and overall design of your portfolio:

Personal Branding

Consistency: Ensure that the portfolio design aligns with your overall personal branding, including your business cards, website, and other marketing materials. This helps in creating a cohesive and professional image.

Color Scheme: Choose a color scheme that represents your style and the message you want to convey. While black can be elegant, professional and sophisticated, other colors might better reflect your creative identity.

Type of Work

Design Style: Your portfolio should visually communicate the type of work you do. For instance, if you specialize in vibrant, colorful illustrations, a portfolio with a bold and colorful design might be more appropriate. Consider a small colorful icon on the cover that reflects your style.

Target Audience: Consider the preferences of your target audience. Corporate clients might appreciate a more subdued, professional look, while creative industries might be more open to bold and innovative designs.

Practical Considerations

Legibility: Ensure that text and images are easy to read and view. High contrast between the background and text, as well as clear images, is essential.

Aesthetic Appeal: The design should be visually appealing and engaging without overshadowing the work being showcased. The portfolio itself should be a testament to your design skills.

Examples of Diverse Portfolio Designs

Minimalist Design: A clean and simple design with ample white space can highlight your work effectively. This style often uses neutral colors, including black, white, and gray or soft, earthy tones.

Bold and Colorful: If your work is creative and vibrant, using bright colors and dynamic layouts can make your portfolio stand out.

Thematic Design: Tailor the design to match the theme of your work. For instance, a nature-themed portfolio could incorporate earthy tones and organic shapes.

Presenting 3-D Projects in Your Portfolio

Presenting 3D work in a portfolio requires careful consideration and should be related to your career goals and the preferences of your target audience. Never include pieces in your portfolio just because you "like" them.

Here are some considerations to help you decide:

1. High-Quality Renders: Use high-quality renders or photographs to accurately showcase the details, textures, and materials of your 3D designs. Ensure that the images are well-lit, properly framed, and highlight the key features.

2. Multiple Views: Include multiple views of each 3D design to provide a comprehensive understanding of the object from different angles. Show front, back, side, inside, top, and bottom views, as well as close-up shots of specific details or components, especially in packaging designs.

3. Contextualization: Place your 3D designs in context to help viewers understand how they would be used or experienced in the real world. This could include placing products in a virtual environment, integrating them into a scene or setting, or showing them alongside related objects or elements, perhaps on a retail shelf.

4. Process Documentation: Include process documentation to demonstrate your design process, from initial concept sketches and ideation to final renders or prototypes. This provides insights into your creative thinking, problem-solving approach, and technical skills.

5. Interactive Elements: If possible, incorporate interactive elements into your portfolio to allow viewers to explore your 3D designs in more detail. This could include interactive 3D models, rotating views, or clickable hotspots to highlight specific features.

6. Animation or Video: Create animations or videos of your 3D designs in action to showcase their functionality, movement, or use. This adds dynamism and engagement to your portfolio and allows viewers to see how your designs behave in real-time.

7. Physical Prototypes/Mockups: If applicable, include photographs or descriptions of physical prototypes or models created from your 3D designs. This demonstrates your ability to translate digital concepts into tangible objects and showcases your hands-on craftsmanship skills, such as in packaging.

8. Descriptive Text: Provide descriptive text or captions for each 3D design to provide context, explain the concept or inspiration behind the design, and highlight key features or functionalities.

The decision of whether to include three-dimensional work, like package design, in a separate section of your portfolio, depends on various factors. These factors include the amount and variety of 3D work you have, the overall structure and organization of your portfolio, and the preferences of your target audience. Ultimately, the choice should be based on what serves your goals best, highlights your strengths, and appeals to your target audience. Try out different approaches and seek feedback from peers, mentors, or industry professionals.

Who is the target audience for my portfolio?

When evaluating your design portfolio, it is crucial to identify and understand your target audience. This ensures that your portfolio aligns with their expectations and showcases your skills in the best possible light.

Here are the key groups to consider:

1. Potential Employers:

Focus: They are looking for evidence of your skills, creativity, and experience.

What to Showcase: Include diverse projects that highlight your versatility and depth in design. Show your ability to solve problems, meet deadlines, and collaborate effectively.

Details: Provide clear and proofread project descriptions, your role in each project, and the outcomes achieved.

2. Clients:

Focus: Clients want to see how your design solutions can meet their needs and add value to their projects and brand.

What to Showcase: Highlight projects similar to the work the client needs. Show your process from concept to final product, emphasizing how you address client briefs and feedback.

Details: Include testimonials or case studies that demonstrate successful collaborations and satisfied clients.

3. Collaborators:

Focus: Collaborators, such as other designers, agencies, or creative professionals, look for synergy in styles and methodologies.

What to Showcase: Include projects that demonstrate your ability to work within a team and your collaborative spirit. Highlight your contributions to joint projects and your flexibility in different roles.

Details: Mention tools, techniques, and methodologies you are proficient in that might align with their practices.

4. Peers and Mentors:

Focus: This group can provide valuable feedback and guidance for improving your work.

What to Showcase: Share a mix of your best work and pieces you feel could benefit from critique. Show a range of skills and be open to feedback.

Details: Be clear about the context of each project and the specific areas where you seek feedback.

5. Academic and Professional Reviewers:

Focus: For those in academia or professional organizations evaluating your portfolio, they look for technical proficiency, creativity, and adherence to industry standards.

What to Showcase: Include projects that reflect both your creative thinking and technical skills. Show your knowledge of design principles, tools, and trends.

Details: Provide detailed process documentation and explain your design decisions and the outcomes.

Remember that to effectively communicate your strengths and meet the expectations of those who will view your portfolio, it's important to understand and define your target audience when assembling your design portfolio.

PRACTICAL TIPS

Tailor Your Portfolio: Depending on the audience, tailor the content and presentation of your portfolio. For example, if applying for a job, focus on projects relevant to the job description.

Organize Thoughtfully: Make it easy for the viewer to navigate your portfolio. Use clear categories, and make sure the most relevant work is easy to find.

Update Regularly: Keep your portfolio current with your latest and best work. Remove outdated or less impressive projects.

Your Résumé: Refine. Refine. Refine.

To improve your chances of success, customize your resume for every job application. Emphasize skills, experiences, and accomplishments that directly align with the specific job requirements. Carefully read the job description to understand the requirements and include relevant keywords from the description to demonstrate your suitability for the position. Various sources, such as resume builder websites, Microsoft Word templates, online resources, graphic design platforms, and your school's career services office offer resume formats that can be accessed online.

Strategies for emphasizing relevant experience, skills, and achievements:

Tailor Your Résumé to the Job: Customize your résumé for each job application by emphasizing relevant skills, experiences, and achievements that align with the specific job requirements. Use keywords from the job description to demonstrate that you're a good fit for the position.

Choose a Clean and Professional Design: Opt for a clean and professional layout that is easy to read and visually appealing. Use a simple font, such as Arial or Times New Roman, and stick to a consistent format throughout your resume. Avoid using excessive colors or decorative elements that may distract from the content.

Start with a Strong Summary or Objective Statement: Begin your résumé with a brief summary or objective statement that highlights your key qualifications and career goals. This section should provide a snapshot of your skills, experiences, and what you offer to potential employers.

Highlight Key Skills and Achievements: Create a dedicated section to showcase your key skills and achievements relevant to the job you're applying for. Use bullet points to list your skills and accomplishments in a clear and concise manner, focusing on quantifiable results whenever possible.

Use Action Verbs and Quantify Achievements: When describing your experiences and accomplishments, use action verbs to start each bullet point and quantify your achievements whenever possible. For example, instead of saying "Responsible for managing social media accounts," you could say "Managed social media accounts with over 10,000 followers, resulting in a 20 percent increase in engagement."

Provide Relevant Work Experience: Start by listing your work experience in reverse chronological order, beginning with your most recent position. For each position, include the job title, company name, location, and dates of employment. Also, provide a brief description of your responsibilities and accomplishments.

Include Education and Certifications: Don't forget to include your educational background, including your degree, major, university name, and graduation date. If applicable, include any certifications, professional development courses, or workshops that showcase your expertise in specific areas.

Add a Section for Additional Information: Consider adding a section for additional information, such as relevant hobbies, volunteer work, or languages spoken. This can provide employers with additional insights into your personality, interests, and skills outside of your professional experience.

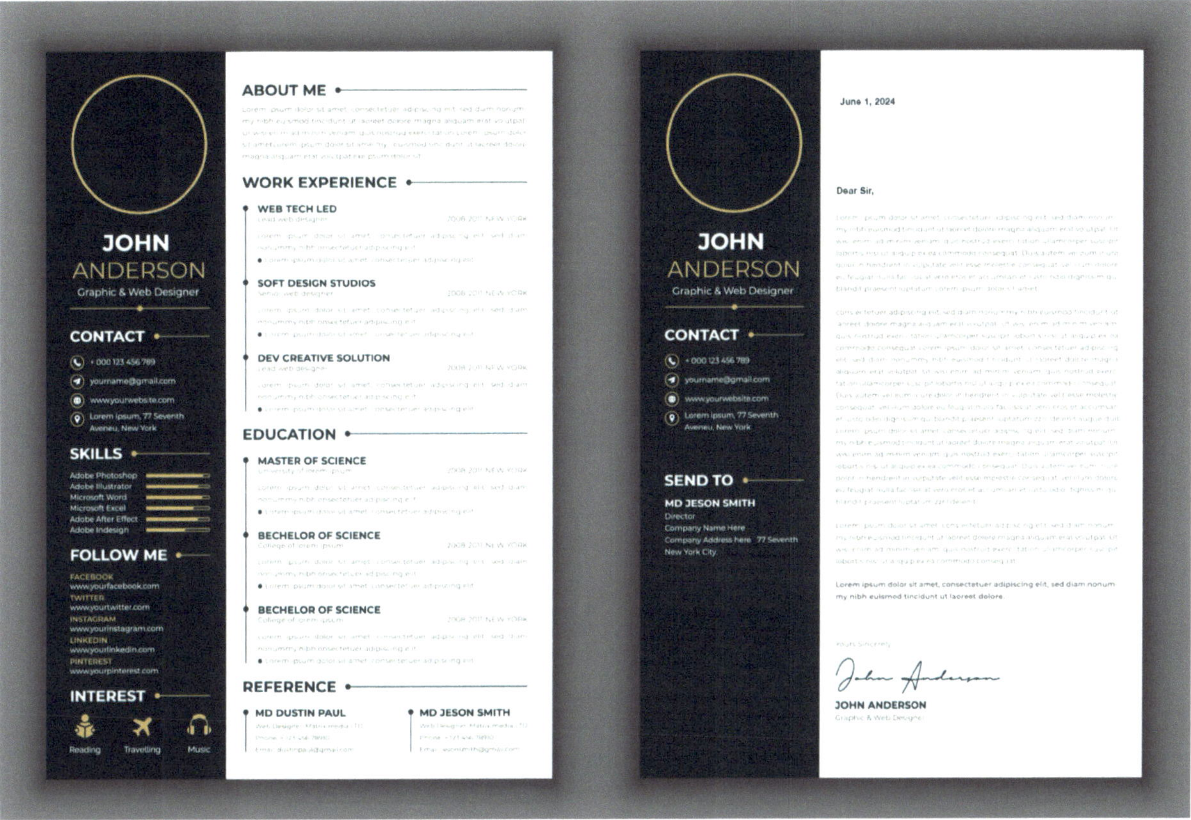

Modern-styled résumé layout with cover letter, showing a very consistent layout and cohesive look. (vecteezy.com).

***The Infographic Résumé:** Infographic résumés are a valuable asset in demonstrating creativity, design abilities, and the talent for presenting information visually. They are especially advantageous in creative and digital industries, startups, and any field that places high importance on visual communication. However, it is crucial to carefully consider the industry and specific role before deciding to utilize an infographic résumé.

Proofread Carefully: Before submitting your résumé, be sure to proofread it carefully to catch any spelling and grammatical errors. It's a good idea to have a friend, family member, or colleague review your résumé as well to catch any mistakes you might have missed. It is acceptable if the résumé information spans across two pages, it is old school to think an entire résumé should be on one page.

Save and Submit in the Right Format: Save your résumé as a PDF file to ensure that formatting remains consistent across different devices and platforms. When submitting your résumé, follow the employer's instructions regarding format and file naming conventions.

*The Infographic résumé stands out and helps differentiate oneself from other candidates in competitive fields, and should not be too crowded. On first impression an infographic résumé creates a strong visual impact and leaves a memorable first impression on recruiters by directly displaying design and layout skills, particularly for roles that require such expertise. This type of résumé effectively communicates key information, making it easier for recruiters to quickly assess qualifications and experience *(see example on the following page).*

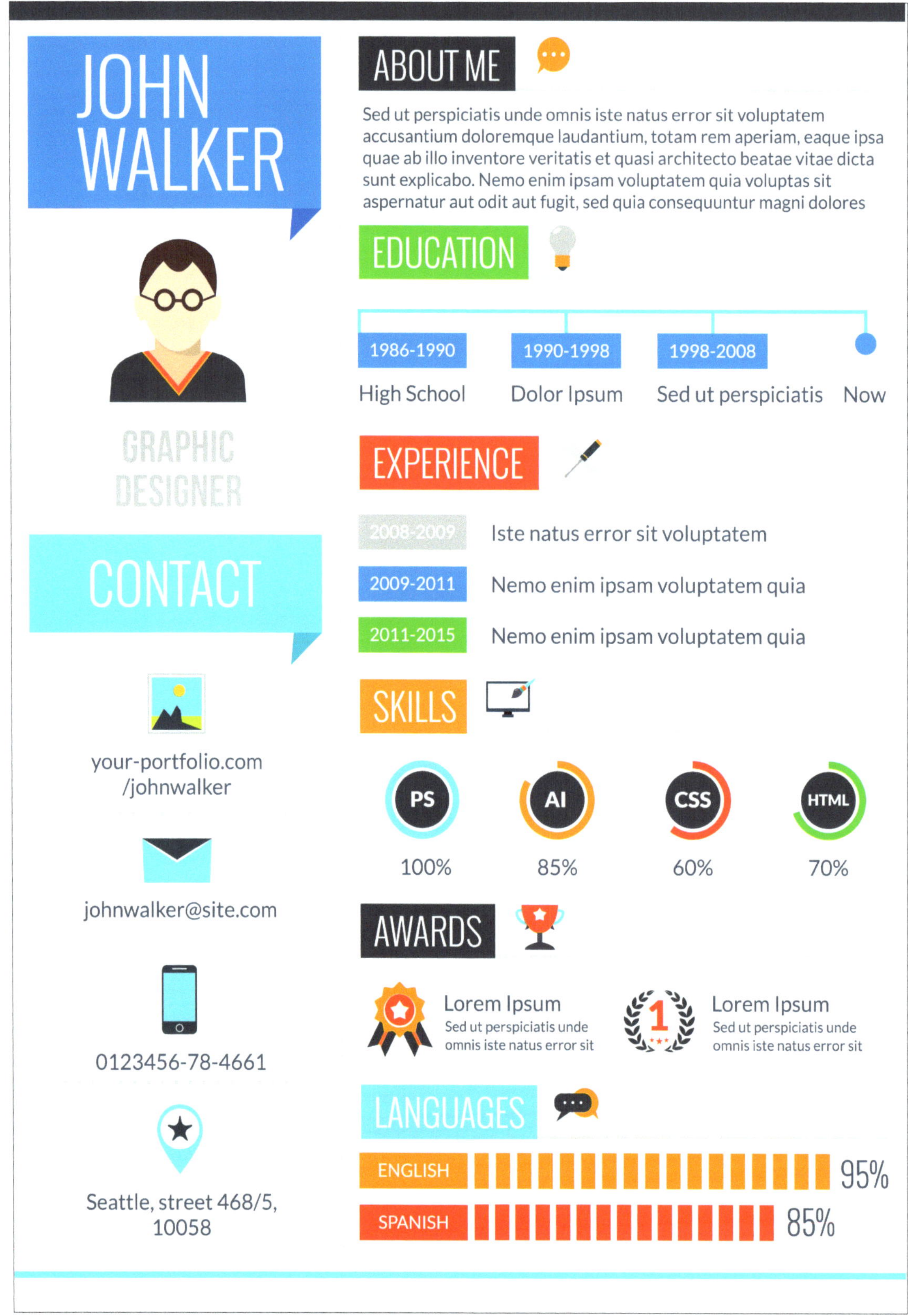

This infographic resume quickly and effectively communicates key information making it easier for recruiters to easily assess qualifications, experience, and determine strengths in specific areas.

BENEFITS OF A COVER LETTER

Although cover letters are not always necessary for a job application, and there are both benefits and potential drawbacks to consider for each choice, a cover letter can greatly enhance your chances and leave a positive impact on potential employers. If a cover letter is optional or not commonly required for the positions you are applying to, focusing on other aspects of your application, such as your résumé and portfolio, may be more beneficial.

Here are some reasons why cover letters are beneficial:

Personalized Introduction: A cover letter allows you to introduce yourself to the hiring manager in a personalized manner. It provides context for your application and highlights your enthusiasm for the position and the company.

Showcasing Fit: A well-written cover letter gives you the opportunity to explain why you are the perfect fit for the role. It allows you to demonstrate how your skills, experiences, and qualifications align with the job requirements and company culture.

Addressing Gaps or Concerns: If there are any gaps in your résumé or aspects of your background that may raise questions, a cover letter enables you to address them proactively and provide explanations or context.

Demonstrating Communication Skills: Writing a compelling cover letter showcases your ability to communicate effectively and express your thoughts clearly and persuasively. This is a valuable skill in any position.

Differentiating Yourself: In a competitive job market, a well-crafted cover letter can help you stand out from other candidates by showcasing your personality, enthusiasm, and unique qualifications.

While cover letters are not always mandatory, they provide an opportunity to make a memorable impression and offer additional context and information that may not be evident from your résumé alone. It is generally a good idea to include a cover letter unless the job posting specifically states otherwise. If you are uncertain whether to include a cover letter, it is best to err on the side of caution and include one to demonstrate your interest and professionalism.

Defining your unique brand as a graphic designer

This is a complex process that involves understanding your design style, core values, personality, and the qualities that make you stand out in the industry. This introspective journey requires identifying the key elements that align with your creative vision and professional ethos. By clearly articulating these aspects, you can create a cohesive and compelling brand identity that not only showcases your talents and approach but also attracts clients and collaborators who resonate with your vision and appreciate your contributions to the field.

Strategies to help you define your brand identity:

1. Take time to contemplate your design style, strengths, and areas of interest. Consider the projects you enjoy working on, your preferred design aesthetics, and the design elements or techniques that resonate with you the most.

2. Clarify Your Values: Determine your core values and beliefs as a designer. What principles guide your work and decision-making process? Consider values such as creativity, innovation, collaboration, integrity, sustainability, or social responsibility that are important to you and reflect them in your brand identity.

3. Find Your Niche: Identify your specialization within graphic design. What specific areas or industries are you passionate about? Whether it's branding, illustration, web design, motion graphics, or another area, defining your niche can help you differentiate yourself and attract clients who are seeking your expertise.

4. Create a Mood Board: Compile a mood board of visual inspiration, including design examples, color palettes, typography, and imagery that align with your design style and personality. Use the mood board as a reference to define and communicate your brand aesthetic.

5. Seek Feedback: Request feedback from peers, mentors, clients, or collaborators on your design work and personal brand. Ask for their impressions of your design style, strengths, and areas for improvement. Their insights can provide valuable perspective and help refine your brand identity.

6. Develop Your Personal Story: Craft a compelling personal story that communicates who you are as a designer, what motivates you, and what sets you apart from others in the field. Share your journey, experiences, and unique perspective to connect with your audience on a deeper level.

7. Maintain Consistent Visual Branding: Establish a consistent visual identity across your portfolio, website, social media profiles, business cards, and other marketing materials. Use consistent colors, typography, imagery, and design elements to reinforce your brand identity and create a cohesive brand experience.

8. Communicate Your Values and Personality: Clearly communicate your values, personality, and design approach in your branding materials, website copy, and social media posts. Use language and tone that reflect your authentic voice and resonate with your target audience.

9. Showcase Your Portfolio: Curate and showcase your best work in your portfolio to demonstrate your skills, style, and range as a designer. Select projects that align with your brand identity and highlight your unique strengths and capabilities.

Stay True to Yourself: Lastly, stay true to yourself and your unique vision as a designer. Avoid trying to imitate someone else's style or conforming to industry trends if they don't align with your authentic self. Embrace your uniqueness and let it shine through in your work and personal brand.

By implementing these strategies, you can define your unique brand identity as a graphic designer and effectively communicate your style, values, and personality to your audience. This will help you attract the right clients, collaborators, and opportunities that align with your brand and vision.

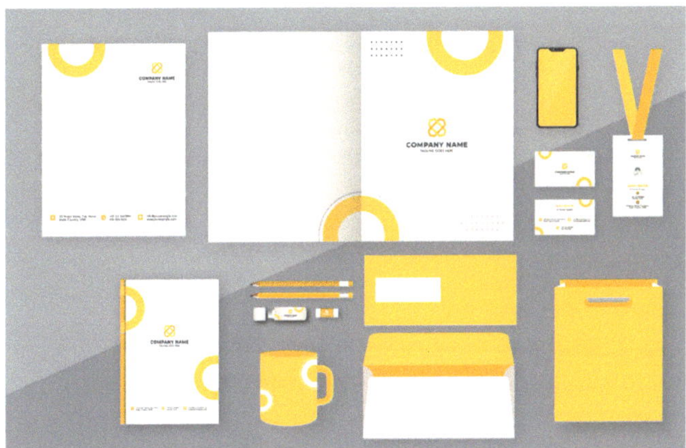

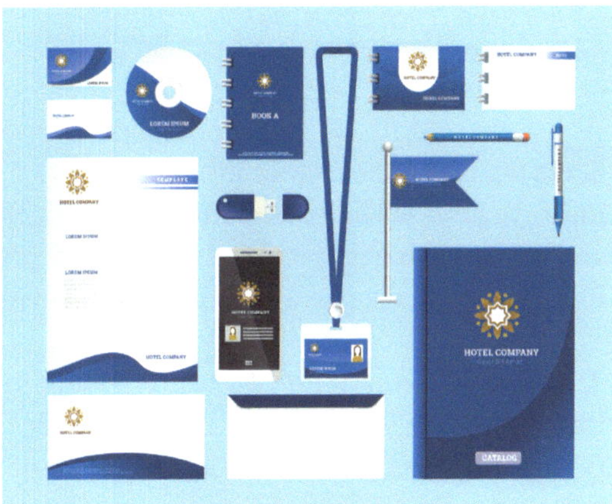

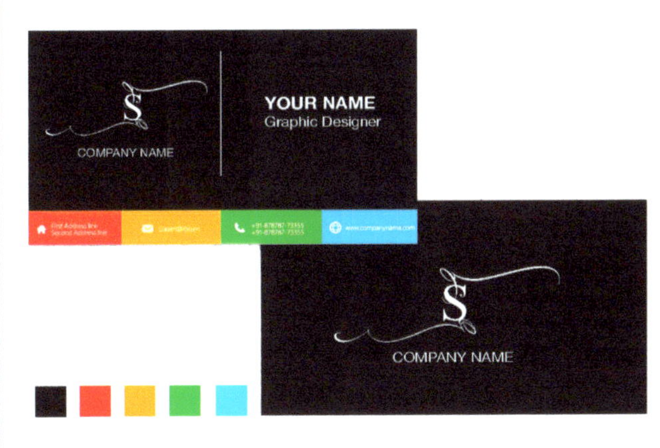

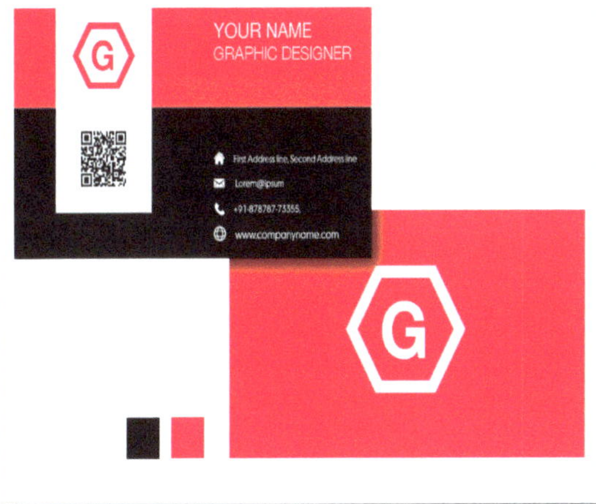

Above left / right - *Consistent visual branding across letterhead, business cards, and other marketing materials.*
Below - *Begin with your brand identity and design your business card first, to hand to prospective clients. Design your letterhead. Select a color scheme that reflects your style, and projects an image of how you would like to be be seen. This means careful selection of colors, typography, and imagery that reinforces your brand identity in a consistent way.*

Creating an Online Presence:

Establishing a professional online presence as a graphic designer is essential for showcasing your work, connecting with clients and collaborators, showcasing your services and growing your network within the industry. Have your brand identity ready so it can be incorporated into all of your online platforms to create a cohesive brand experience for visitors.

Here are some practical tips to help you build and maintain a strong online presence:

1. Create a Professional Website: Invest in creating a professional website to serve as your online portfolio. Use a clean and user-friendly design that showcases your best work, provides information about your services, and includes contact details for potential clients to reach you. Platforms like Squarespace, Wix, or WordPress offer easy-to-use website templates for designers.

2. Showcase Your Best Work: Curate your portfolio to showcase your best and most relevant work. Include a diverse range of projects that highlight your skills, expertise, and versatility as a designer. Provide context for each project, including client objectives, your role, and any notable achievements or outcomes.

3. Optimize for Search Engines (SEO): Optimize your website and portfolio for search engines to improve your visibility and attract more traffic. Use relevant keywords, meta tags, and descriptive titles and captions to help potential clients find you online. Regularly update your content and engage with industry-related keywords to improve your search rankings.

4. Maintain Consistent Branding: Maintain consistent branding across your online platforms, including your website, social media profiles, and promotional materials. Use consistent colors, typography, imagery, and messaging to reinforce your brand identity and create a cohesive brand experience for visitors.

5. Engage on Social Media: Utilize social media platforms such as Instagram, Behance, Dribbble, and LinkedIn to showcase your work, connect with other designers, and engage with potential clients. Share your latest projects, design insights, industry news, and behind-the-scenes glimpses to build your online presence and attract followers.

6. Participate in Online Communities: Join online design communities, forums, and groups where you can network with other designers, share knowledge, and seek feedback on your work. Engage actively in discussions, offer valuable insights, and contribute to the community to establish yourself as a knowledgeable and respected member.

7. Start a Design Blog: Consider starting a design blog on your website where you can share your thoughts, insights, and experiences as a graphic designer. Write about design trends, techniques, case studies, or personal projects to showcase your expertise and provide valuable content for your audience.

8. Offer Free Resources or Tutorials: Share free resources, templates, or tutorials related to graphic design on your website or social media platforms. Providing valuable content demonstrates your expertise, generosity, and willingness to help others, which can attract more followers and potential clients to your online presence.

9. Collect Testimonials and Recommendations: Collect testimonials and recommendations from satisfied clients or collaborators and display them prominently on your website. Positive reviews and endorsements from others can help build trust and credibility with potential clients and reassure them of your professionalism and quality of work.

10. Stay Active and Engaged: Regularly update your website and social media profiles with new content, projects, and updates to keep your audience engaged and informed. Respond promptly to inquiries, comments, and messages from potential clients or collaborators to demonstrate your professionalism and responsiveness.

By implementing these practical tips, you can establish a professional online presence as a graphic designer, showcase your work effectively, and attract more clients and opportunities within the industry. Consistency, quality, and authenticity are key to building a strong online brand that reflects your skills, expertise, and personality as a designer.

Setting Yourself Apart

Setting yourself apart from other graphic designers, especially as a freelancer involves honing your skills, developing a unique style, and effectively marketing yourself.

Here are some strategies to help you stand out:

1. Develop a Unique Style

Find Your Niche: Specialize in a particular area of design, such as branding, web design, illustration, or motion graphics.

Create a Signature Style: Develop a distinctive visual style that is recognizable and consistent across your work.

2. Build a Strong Portfolio

Showcase Diverse Projects: Include a variety of projects that demonstrate your range and versatility.

Quality Over Quantity: Focus on presenting your best work, even if it means having fewer pieces in your portfolio.

Case Studies: Provide detailed case studies that explain your design process, the challenges you faced, and the solutions you implemented.

3. Stay Updated with Industry Trends

Continuous Learning: Stay current with design trends, new tools, and technologies by taking online courses, attending workshops, and reading industry blogs.

Experiment with New Techniques: Regularly try out new design methods and tools to keep your skills fresh and innovative.

4. Enhance Your Skills

Learn New Tools: Master various design software and tools beyond the standard ones like Adobe Creative Suite. Consider learning about 3D design, animation, or coding.

Improve Soft Skills: Work on communication, project management, and client relationship skills.

5. Network and Collaborate

Join Professional Communities: Participate in design communities, both online and offline. Attend industry events, webinars, and conferences.

Collaborate with Other Creatives: Work on projects with other designers, artists, and professionals from different fields, both locally and nationally to gain new perspectives and skills.

6. Market Yourself Effectively

Create a Professional Website: Ensure your website is well-designed, easy to navigate, and showcases your best work.

Use Social Media: Share your work on platforms like Instagram, Behance, Dribbble, and LinkedIn. Engage with the community by commenting on others' work and participating in design challenges.

SEO and Blogging: Optimize your website for search engines and consider writing blog posts about design trends, tutorials, and case studies.

7. Offer Exceptional Client Service

Understand Client Needs: Listen carefully to your clients' requirements and provide solutions that align with their goals.

Timely Delivery and Professionalism: Meet deadlines, communicate effectively, and maintain a professional demeanor in all interactions, including setting timelines, defining project scope, and coordinating with team members or clients.

8. Get Certified and Recognized

Certifications: Obtain certifications from reputable design organizations or software companies. This includes staying updated on industry trends, mastering new design tools, and honing specialized skills.

Awards and Competitions: Enter design competitions and strive to earn awards. This can provide recognition and credibility. If you're happy with your designs don't hesitate to enter them in annual design competitions. There are several competitions.

9. Seek Feedback and Refine

Request Feedback: Regularly ask for feedback from peers, mentors, and clients to identify areas for improvement in your design work. Explore strategies for leveraging mentorship opportunities and learning from experienced professionals in the field.

Refine and Improve: Continuously refine your skills and portfolio based on the feedback you receive. Engage in continuous learning and skill development in the ever-evolving field of graphic design. Stay updated on industry trends, mastering new design tools, and honing specialized skills.

By combining these strategies, you can distinguish yourself from other graphic designers and build a successful, recognizable brand in the industry. But, you must be committed, dedicated, consistent, and goal-oriented, and most of all fearless. Ask for help and advice when you feel that you must. Believe in yourself and never let anyone else determine your course but you.

Should I show nonprofit work in my portfolio?

There is significant value in engaging in nonprofit work. It provides an opportunity for you to contribute positively to your community, build a diverse portfolio, gain unique experiences, and network with professionals who share similar values. Additionally, participating in nonprofit work can enhance your skills and demonstrate your commitment to social responsibility, thereby making you a more attractive candidate to potential employers.

Here are some steps to effectively leverage nonprofit work:

1. Identify Causes You Care About

Choose Causes that Matter: Select nonprofit organizations or causes that align with your personal values and interests. This ensures that you are genuinely passionate about the work you do.

2. Reach Out to Nonprofits

Research Organizations: Look for nonprofits that could benefit from your skills. Smaller organizations may have more urgent design needs and limited budgets.

Offer Your Services: Contact these organizations with a proposal, explaining how your design skills can help them achieve their goals. Clearly state what you can offer and any specific projects you have in mind.

3. Create High-Impact Work

Focus on Quality: Treat nonprofit projects with the same level of professionalism and creativity as you would for paying clients. Producing high-quality work will reflect positively on you.

Innovative Solutions: Provide innovative design solutions that have a significant impact on the organization's visibility and engagement.

4. Document the Process

Case Studies: Develop detailed case studies for each nonprofit project. Include the initial problem, your design process, and the outcomes. Highlight any positive feedback or measurable impact your work had.

Testimonials: Request testimonials from nonprofit leaders or stakeholders. Positive endorsements from nonprofit organizations can be powerful additions to your portfolio.

5. Leverage Your Work for Publicity

Press Releases: Coordinate with the nonprofit to issue press releases about your work. Highlight the collaboration and its impact on the community.

Social Media: Share your nonprofit projects on your social media platforms, tagging the organizations and using relevant hashtags to increase visibility.

6. Network Through Nonprofit Work

Attend Events: Participate in nonprofit events and networking opportunities. These events can introduce you to potential clients, collaborators, and industry leaders.

Collaborate with Other Volunteers: Work closely with other volunteers and professionals involved in the nonprofit. These connections can lead to new opportunities and referrals.

7. Showcase Your Nonprofit Work

Portfolio Inclusion: Feature your nonprofit work prominently in your portfolio. Emphasize the impact and the story behind each project.

Website and Blog: Write blog posts about your nonprofit projects on your website, detailing your experiences and the outcomes.

8. Gain Recognition Through Awards

Enter Competitions: Submit your nonprofit work to design competitions and awards. Many design awards have categories for social impact and nonprofit work.

Local Recognition: Look for local or regional awards that acknowledge contributions to the community. This can increase your visibility in your local area.

9. Use Nonprofit Work as a Learning Experience

Skill Development: Use nonprofit projects as an opportunity to explore new techniques, tools, or design approaches. This can help you grow as a designer.

Feedback and Improvement: Utilize feedback from nonprofit clients to improve your work and gain a deeper understanding of different perspectives and needs.

10. Highlight the Impact

Quantifiable Results: Whenever possible, highlight the measurable impact of your work, such as increased donations, higher engagement rates, or expanded reach.

Visual Storytelling: Use before-and-after visuals, info graphics, and compelling narratives to tell the story of your nonprofit projects.

By integrating nonprofit work into your portfolio, you not only contribute positively to causes you care about but also demonstrate your commitment, versatility, and impact as a graphic designer. This approach can significantly enhance your reputation and open up new professional opportunities. Nonprofit projects do have a good feeling of satisfaction and giving back to communities and those in need.

CHAPTER TWO
CRAFTING JOB APPLICATIONS

Crafting Job Applications

Tailoring your job application materials to specific job postings is essential for effectively highlighting your qualifications and standing out from the competition.

Here are some tips to help you customize your application materials for specific job postings and set yourself apart from other applicants.

1. Carefully read the job description: Take the time to thoroughly read and understand the job description and requirements provided by the employer. Pay close attention to the qualifications, skills, and experiences they are looking for in potential candidates.

2. Highlight relevant skills and experiences: Identify the key qualifications and requirements outlined in the job description. Make sure to highlight your skills and experiences that demonstrate your ability to meet these requirements. Customize your resume, cover letter, and portfolio to showcase your most relevant achievements and experiences that are related to the job.

3. Use keywords from the job posting: Incorporate keywords and phrases from the job posting into your resume and cover letter. By doing so, you ensure that your application aligns with the employer's needs and stands out to applicant tracking systems (ATS). Additionally, using industry-specific terminology and buzzwords that demonstrate your familiarity with the field can be beneficial.

4. Quantify your achievements: Whenever possible, provide concrete evidence of your skills and impact by quantifying your achievements and accomplishments. Use numbers, percentages, or metrics to quantify the results of your work and demonstrate your effectiveness in previous roles.

5. Tailor your cover letter: Customize your cover letter to specifically address the requirements and qualifications outlined in the job posting. Explain how your skills and experiences make you a strong fit for the position and express your genuine interest in working for the company.

6. Include relevant projects, work samples, or portfolio pieces: Include projects, work samples, or portfolio pieces that are relevant to the job and demonstrate your skills and expertise. Choose examples that highlight your best work and align with the employer's needs and industry.

7. Research the company: Take the time to research the company, including its culture, values, and recent projects or initiatives. Use this knowledge to customize your application materials. Show genuine interest in the company and how you can contribute to its success.

8. Proofread carefully: Before submitting your application, thoroughly proofread your résumé, cover letter, and any other materials. Make sure they are error-free, with no typos or grammatical mistakes. Attention to detail is crucial, and errors can harm your professionalism and credibility.

9. Follow up after applying: It is advisable to send a polite email or make a phone call to follow up on your application. In this communication, if still interested, express your ongoing interest in the position and ask about the status of your application. Remember to always proofread and spellcheck before sending. This will show your enthusiasm and proactive attitude towards the hiring process.

Sample Follow-Up Emails:

Dear [Hiring Manager's Name],

I am following up on my recent application for the [Job Title] position at [Company Name]. I submitted my application on [Date] and would like to express my continued interest in joining your team. I believe my skills and experiences align perfectly with the qualifications specified in the job description.

I would greatly appreciate any updates you can provide regarding the status of my application or the subsequent steps in the hiring process. If you require any additional information or documentation from me, please let me know.

Thank you for considering my application. I am enthusiastic about the possibility of contributing to [Company Name] and look forward to discussing how my skills and experiences can benefit your team.

Warm regards,

[Your Name]
[Your Contact Information]

Dear [Hiring Manager's Name],

I recently applied for the [Job Title] position at [Company Name] and wanted to follow up on its status.

I believe my skills and experiences align well with the job requirements and I am eager to bring my expertise in [specific skill or area] to [Company Name]. I hope to have the opportunity to discuss how I can contribute to your goals.

Thank you for considering my application. I look forward to the possibility of discussing this opportunity with you. Please let me know if there are any additional materials or information I can provide.

Sincerely,
[Your Name]

By following these tips and tailoring your job application to match specific job postings, you can successfully highlight your qualifications, distinguish yourself from other applicants, and improve your chances of securing an interview and ultimately getting hired. Both follow-up emails are short, polite, and to the point, ensuring you remain professional while expressing your continued interest in the position.

CHAPTER THREE
THE JOB INTERVIEW

Preparing for the Job Interview

Include a variety of projects that demonstrate your range and versatility in your portfolio, focusing on presenting your best work, even if it means having fewer pieces in your portfolio. Provide detailed case studies that explain your design process, the challenges you faced, and the solutions you implemented.

Review Your Portfolio: Make sure your portfolio is up-to-date and organized. Be prepared to discuss each piece in detail, focusing on your role, the process, and the outcomes.

Practice Common Interview Questions: Practice answering common interview questions, both technical and behavioral. This will help you articulate your thoughts clearly and confidently.

Research the Company: Learn about the company's history, mission, values, and recent projects. Be ready to explain why you want to work there and how you can contribute.

Prepare Questions: Have a list of questions ready to ask the interviewer about the role, team structure, company culture, and expectations.

During the Interview

Show Enthusiasm: Demonstrate your passion for design and enthusiasm for the role.

Be Professional: Dress appropriately, arrive on time, and maintain a positive and professional demeanor.

Communicate Clearly:
Speak clearly and confidently, and make sure to listen carefully to the interviewer's questions and comments. If you brought a "leave-behind" you will want to give it give it to interviewers nearing the end or at the end a job interview.

After the Interview

Follow Up: Send a thank-you email to express your appreciation for the opportunity to interview and reiterate your interest in the position. Mention any specific points from the interview that particularly resonated with you.

By preparing thoroughly and presenting yourself confidently, you can make a strong impression and increase your chances of landing the graphic design position.

Types and/or Styles of Interviews

When interviewing for a graphic design position, there are various interview styles that assess your creative skills and professional fit within the company. It is important to research to be prepared.

Common types and styles of interviews include:

1. Portfolio Review:

Purpose: Evaluate your design skills, creativity, and ability to explain your design process.

Format: Present your portfolio and discuss the context, objectives, challenges, and outcomes of selected projects.

Preparation: Choose diverse projects that showcase your best work and demonstrate a range of skills. Be ready to discuss design decisions, tools used, and impact of your work.

2. Technical Interview:

Purpose: Assess proficiency with design software and technical skills.

Format: Complete a design task using specific software, such as Adobe Creative Suite, Sketch, or Figma. Task may be a live exercise or take-home assignment.

Preparation: Practice using relevant software and brush up on specific skills mentioned in the job description.

3. Behavioral Interview:

Purpose: Understand how you handle work situations and fit within the team culture.

Format: Answer questions about past experiences, focusing on how you've handled challenges, collaborated, and managed projects.

Preparation: Use the STAR method (Situation, Task, Action, Result) to structure responses. Reflect on past projects and provide examples highlighting problem-solving skills, teamwork, and adaptability.

4. Creative Interview:

Purpose: Gauge creativity and ability to think on your feet.

Format: Solve hypothetical scenarios or design challenges.

Preparation: Stay updated on design trends and be prepared to brainstorm ideas or sketch concepts quickly.

5. Cultural Fit Interview:

Purpose: Determine alignment with company values and work environment.

Format: Informal conversations about interests, work style, and career goals.

Preparation: Research company culture and reflect on how values and work habits align. Be honest and personable.

6. Panel Interview:

Purpose: Assess communication and presentation skills to a group.

Format: Multiple team members with different roles and perspectives interview you.

Preparation: Practice presenting your portfolio to a group and be ready for diverse questions. Focus on clear communication and be prepared to engage with different viewpoints.

7. Take-Home Assignment

Purpose: This interview evaluates your design process and problem-solving skills over an extended period.

Format: You will receive a design brief and be asked to complete a project within a given time frame.

Preparation: Treat the assignment like a real project. Follow the brief closely, manage your time effectively, and present your work professionally.

8. Video Interview

Purpose: This interview is for initial screening or when in-person interviews are not possible.

Format: This could be a live video call or a pre-recorded interview where you respond to set questions.

Preparation: Ensure a quiet, professional setting with good lighting and a stable Internet connection. Practice speaking clearly and confidently on camera.

Tips For Success:

Research the Company: Understand their design style, products, and recent projects. Tailor your portfolio and examples to align with their work.

Prepare Questions: Show your interest in the role by asking insightful questions about the team, projects, and company goals.

Be Yourself: Authenticity helps interviewers assess your fit for the team. Let your personality and passion for design shine through.

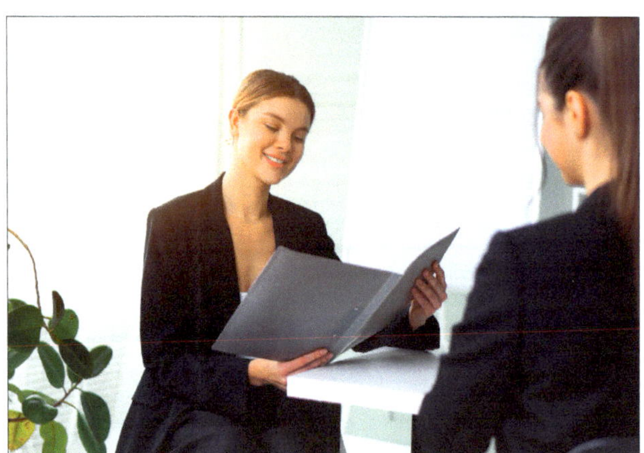

Interview in progress

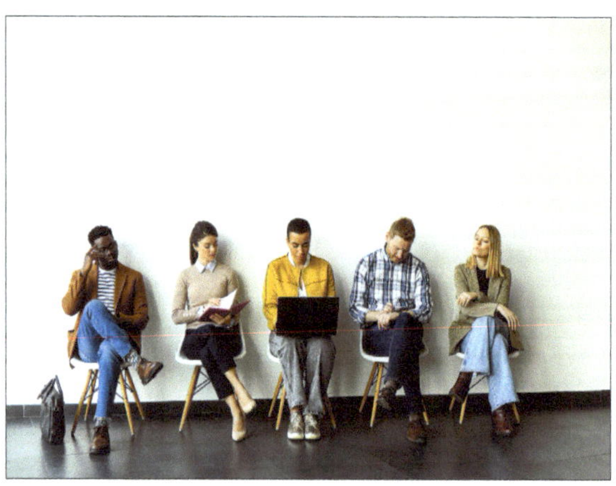

Job applicants await their turn to be interviewed.

The In-Person Interview

So you've finally got the call or email you've been hoping for! Yeah! If you are contacted for a job interview for a graphic design position, you can expect a variety of questions and tasks designed to assess your skills, creativity, and fit for the company as mentioned previously. Some companies also request an initial video introduction before they invite you in for a personal interview.

Here's a breakdown of what you might encounter for an in-person interview:

Interview Stages and Components

Introduction and Background Discussion:

Self-Introduction: Be prepared to introduce yourself and provide a brief overview of your background, education, and work experience.

Portfolio Review: You will likely be asked to present your portfolio. Be ready to discuss your projects, the design process, the tools you used, and the challenges you overcame.

Technical and Design Skills Assessment:

Software Proficiency: Expect questions about your proficiency with design software such as the Adobe Creative Suite (Photoshop, Illustrator, InDesign), Sketch, Figma, or other relevant tools.

Design Challenges: You might be given a design challenge or task to complete during the interview or as a take-home assignment. This could involve creating a logo, a web page layout, or another design element to showcase your skills.

Technical Questions: Be prepared for questions about design principles, typography, color theory, and other technical aspects of graphic design.

Behavioral and Situational Questions:

Teamwork and Collaboration: Questions about how you work in a team, handle feedback, and collaborate with other designers, developers, and clients.

Problem-Solving: Situational questions that assess how you handle tight deadlines, difficult clients, or project challenges.

Career Goals and Motivation: Expect questions about your career aspirations, why you're interested in this particular role, and what you know about the company.

Cultural Fit and Personality Assessment:

Company Culture: Interviewers will assess how well you align with the company's values and culture. Be prepared to discuss what attracts you to the company and how you see yourself fitting in.

Work Ethic and Style: Questions about your work ethic, how you manage your time, and your approach to creativity and innovation.

Listen Carefully to Interview Questions

Listening carefully to interview questions is vital as it allows you to respond appropriately, demonstrates your engagement and professionalism, and helps you determine if the role and company are a good fit for you. By honing your listening skills, you can significantly improve your performance in interviews and increase your chances of success.

Listening carefully to interview questions is crucial for several reasons:

1. Demonstrates Active Engagement

Engagement: Actively listening shows the interviewer that you are fully engaged in the conversation and interested in the role.

Respect: It demonstrates respect for the interviewer's time and effort in conducting the interview.

2. Provides Insight into the Role and Company

Understanding Requirements: Careful listening helps you grasp the specific skills, experiences, and attributes the employer is looking for.

Cultural Fit: It can give you clues about the company culture and values, helping you assess if the organization is a good fit for you.

3. Enables Precise and Relevant Responses

Accuracy: Understanding the questions fully allows you to provide accurate and relevant answers.

Tailoring Responses: You can tailor your responses to highlight the most pertinent aspects of your experience and skills.

4. Reduces Miscommunication

Clarity: Careful listening reduces the risk of misinterpreting questions, which can lead to inappropriate or irrelevant answers.

Follow-up Questions: It helps you formulate clarifying questions if any part of the question is unclear.

5. Highlights Your Communication Skills

Active Listening: Demonstrates your ability to listen actively, a key component of effective communication.

Professionalism: It reflects your professionalism and attention to detail.

6. Builds Rapport

Positive Interaction: Engaging effectively through listening builds rapport with the interviewer, creating a positive impression.

Connection: It can make the conversation flow more smoothly and naturally, making both you and the interviewer more comfortable.

Strategies for Effective Listening During an Interview

Nervousness: Try not to be nervous. Relax.

Focus: Eliminate distractions and focus entirely on the interviewer.

Non-Verbal Cues: Use non-verbal cues like nodding to show you are listening.

Take Notes: If appropriate, take brief notes to help remember key points.

Pause: Take a moment to think before answering to ensure you have understood the question fully.

Ask for Clarification: If a question is unclear, don't hesitate to ask for clarification.

FUNNY INTERVIEW MISHAPS

Don't let any of these scenarios cost you your interview:

Scenario #1: The interview started off with a mishap when, just two minutes into the hour-long interview, they were asked, "tell me how you got here today." Their response was simply, "by bus." It quickly became clear that the question was meant to gauge their career path, not their mode of transportation. They humorously remarked that the remaining 58 minutes felt like going through the motions.

Scenario #2: In another instance, the interviewee was asked if they had a driving license and a car. Without hesitation, they confidently answered "yes." However, their confidence waned when they were further questioned about the cleanliness of their car. They proudly stated that they had recently washed it, only to realize that the interviewer was referring to points on their driving license.

Scenario #3: One particular incident involved someone who had slightly exaggerated their proficiency in French on their CV. Surprisingly, the interviewer began the conversation in fluent French, leaving the interviewee completely bewildered. They admitted that the interview was practically over before they even had a chance to sit down. This serves as a valuable reminder not to fabricate information on your application.

Scenario #4: Lastly, someone revealed that when asked about their background, they inexplicably turned around and started describing what was behind them.

Excerpted from Joe Harker — LADBible/Entertainment

Negotiating Pay During the Interview

Negotiating your compensation during the interview can be challenging but crucial in establishing your value and ensuring fair compensation. This step is critical for graphic designers, as well as many other professions. Job postings may sometimes include a salary range, giving candidates a rough idea of the compensation before applying.

Here are some strategies to effectively negotiate your pay:

1. Conduct thorough research

Market Rates: Research the average salary for entry-level graphic designers in your area using websites like Glassdoor, PayScale, and LinkedIn Salary.

Industry Standards: Understand what is typical for your industry, considering factors such as company size, location, and specific skills.

2. Evaluate your skills and experience

Assess your value: Consider additional skills that you bring to the table, such as proficiency in specific software, experience with various design styles, any internships or freelance work.

Portfolio Strength: Ensure your portfolio is polished and showcases your best work. Highlight projects that demonstrate your ability to deliver quality results.

3. Prepare for the negotiation

Practice negotiation: Role-play negotiation scenarios with a friend or mentor to build your confidence.

Know your worth: Determine a salary range that you believe is fair based on your research and personal value assessment. Have a minimum acceptable salary in mind, but aim for a higher number.

4. Timing is crucial

Wait for the offer: Allow the employer to bring up the salary first. This will help you understand their starting point.

Consider the entire compensation package: Evaluate the benefits, opportunities for growth, work-life balance, and other perks offered in addition to the salary.

5. Clearly and confidently communicate

Maintain professionalism: Approach the negotiation professionally and respectfully. Express gratitude for the offer and enthusiasm for the position.

Use data: Reference your research and the value you bring to the company to justify your salary request.

Stay positive: Frame your request in a positive manner. Instead of saying "I need more money," say "Based on my skills and research on industry standards, I believe a salary of [desired amount] is appropriate."

6. Be prepared for counteroffers

Be flexible: Be willing to negotiate and consider counteroffers. If the employer cannot meet your desired salary, discuss alternative forms of compensation such as bonuses, additional vacation time, or professional development opportunities.

Long-term growth: Inquire about potential salary reviews and raises in the near future. This demonstrates your commitment to growing with the company.

7. Recognize when to decline

Evaluate the offer: If the salary is significantly below your minimum acceptable range and there are no additional benefits to compensate for it, be prepared to politely decline the offer.

Value alignment: Ensure that the company's values and work environment align with your professional goals and personal values.

Example script for negotiation

Employer: "We are pleased to offer you the graphic designer position with a starting salary of $40,000."

You: "Thank you for the offer. I am excited about the opportunity to work with your team. Based on my research and the skills I bring, including proficiency in Adobe Creative Suite and my recent experience with [specific project or skill], I was hoping to discuss a salary in the range of $45,000 to $50,000. Is there flexibility in your budget to accommodate this?"

Additional tips

Document everything: Keep records of all communications related to salary negotiations.

Continual learning: Even after securing a position, continue improving your skills and staying updated with industry trends to position yourself for future raises and promotions.

By thoroughly preparing and approaching the negotiation process with confidence and professionalism, you can effectively negotiate a fair salary as an entry-level graphic designer.

The Interview "Leave-Behind." What is it?

A "leave-behind" is a physical or digital item that you give to interviewers at the end of a job interview. It serves as a tangible reminder of you and your work. For a graphic design position, a leave-behind typically includes samples of your design work, but it can also be a creatively designed item that showcases your skills and personality.

Here's why leave-behinds are significant and how you can effectively use them:

Significance of a Leave-Behind

Memorability

Lasting Impression: A leave-behind helps you stand out by providing something memorable for the interviewers to look at after the interview. It reinforces your presence and leaves a lasting impression.
Visual Reminder: It keeps your work and contact information easily accessible, ensuring you remain top of mind when the decision-making process occurs.

Showcase Skills

Creativity and Skill: It's an opportunity to showcase your creativity, design skills, and attention to detail. A well-designed leave-behind demonstrates your ability to produce high-quality work.
Professionalism: It signals your professionalism and preparedness. A thoughtfully created leave-behind indicates that you go the extra mile.

Portfolio Supplement

Additional Work: It can include work that complements what you presented in your portfolio, offering a broader view of your capabilities.

Tailored Content: You can tailor the content to the specific company or role, highlighting the most relevant projects and skills.

Effective Leave-Behind Ideas

Mini Portfolio:

A compact version of your portfolio with selected works that best represent your skills and align with the job role. Ensure it is well-designed and easy to flip through.

Business Card with a Twist:

A creatively designed business card that includes a QR code linking to your online portfolio or a personalized message for the interviewer.

Branded Items:

Custom-designed items like postcards, bookmarks, or stickers that feature your artwork and contact information.

Booklet or Brochure

A small booklet or brochure that outlines your key projects, design process, and accomplishments. Include visuals, descriptions, and your contact details.

Interactive Digital Leave-Behind:

A USB drive or a QR code linking to an interactive PDF or a special web page designed specifically for the interviewers, showcasing your best work and relevant projects.

TIPS FOR CREATING A LEAVE-BEHIND

Relevance:

Tailor the leave-behind to the company and the job role. Include work that aligns with the company's aesthetic and the position's requirements.

Quality:

Ensure high production quality. Use good materials if it's a physical item and high-resolution images for digital content.

Conciseness:

Keep it concise. A few well-chosen pieces that highlight your strengths are more effective than a comprehensive but overwhelming collection.

Personal Touch:

Add a personal touch, such as a handwritten note or a custom message, to make it more personable and engaging.

By carefully crafting and presenting a leave-behind after your job interview, you can greatly improve your chances of being remembered positively and standing out from other candidates. Some designers choose to create unique and personalized pieces or a one-of-a-kind creative leave-behind for the entire office. Regardless of what you decide to do, make sure that it is both relevant to the job and office, and also memorable. After all, you wouldn't want all your time and effort to end up in the trash once you've left.

Two Examples of Creative Leave-Behinds

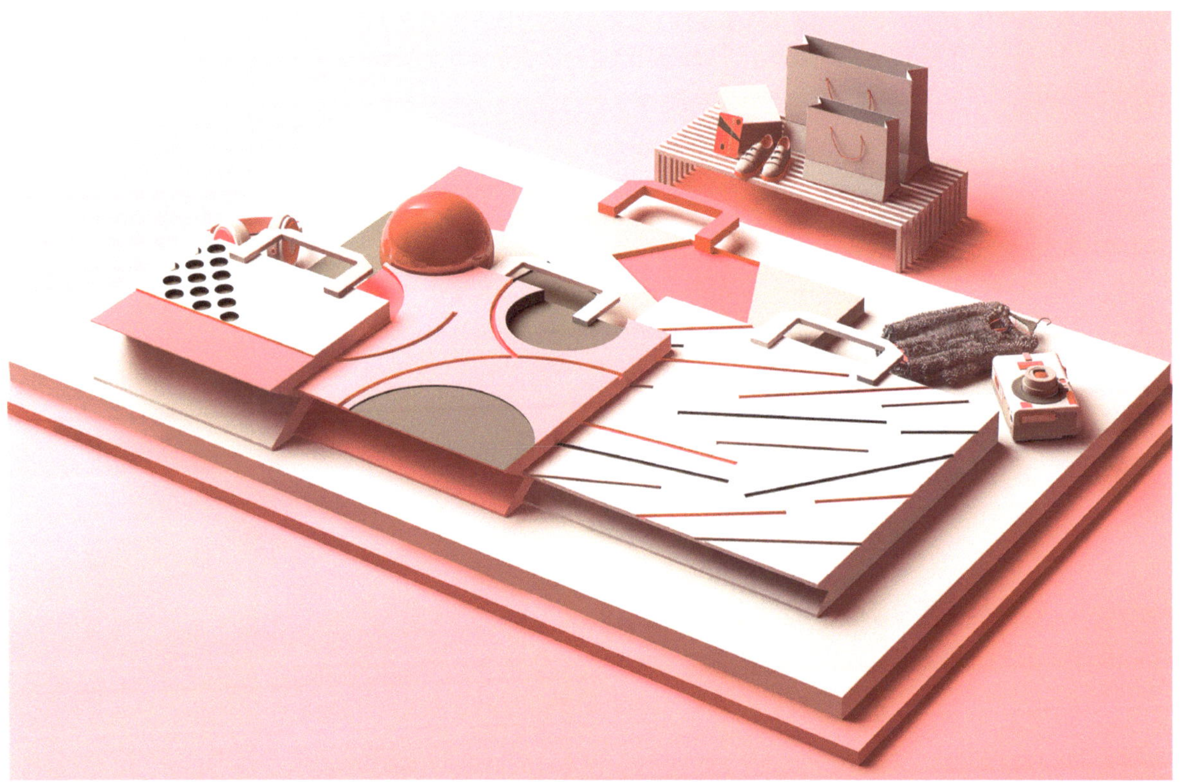

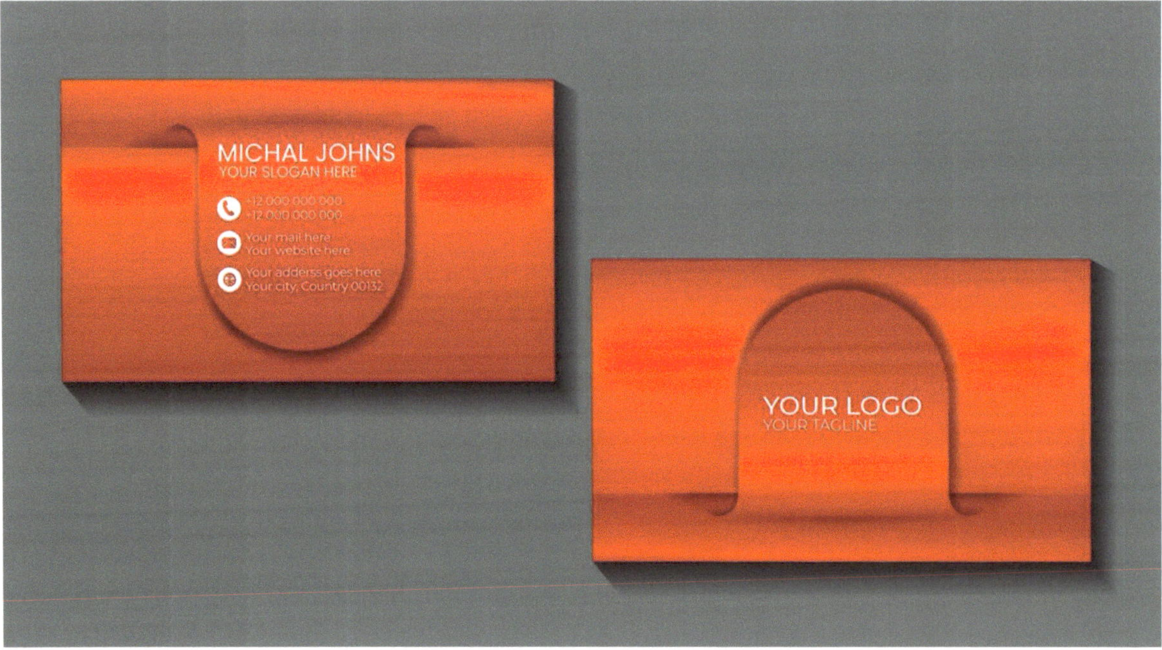

Above: *A very involved and creative 3-D leave-behind best for an office team, perhaps can sit on a table as a converstion piece. This shows meticulous, masterful craftsmanship skills and creative design-thinking. Consider your colors too.*
Below: *A memorable business card holder with your clearly visible logo and contact information. Should be the color of your brand.*

Finding Inspiration for Creative Leave-Behinds

Images of creative leave-behinds such as business cards, brochures, portfolios, or promotional materials, can be done through various resources that offer high-quality images for free.

Here are some websites where you can search for such images:

1. Unsplash

Description: A large collection of high-quality images contributed by photographers worldwide. Free.

Link: Unsplash.com

3. Pixabay

Description: Provides over 1.7 million free stock photos, videos, and illustrations. Good for finding images of different design leave-behinds.

Link: Pixabay.com

4. Freepik

Description: A resource for free vectors, stock photos, PSDs, and icons. Particularly useful for design-related images and mock-ups.

Link: Freepik.com

5. Rawpixel

Description: Offers free high-resolution images and mock-ups, often with an artistic or design-focused approach.

6. Designspiration

Description: A hub for creative inspiration, including design projects. Useful for finding examples of creative leave-behinds.

Link: Designspiration.com

Tips for Using Free Image Resources:

Check Licenses: Always verify the licensing terms for each image to ensure it is free to use, even for commercial purposes.

Attribution: Some sources require attribution. Give proper credit if required.

Search Keywords: Use specific keywords like "business card mock-up," "brochure design," "portfolio showcase," or "promotional materials" to find relevant images.

By using these resources, you can find a wide range of creative and free images that showcase designers' leave-behinds, providing inspiration and examples for your own projects.

CHAPTER FOUR
NAVIGATING THE JOB MARKET

Navigating the job market as a graphic designer

This involves several key steps that can increase your chances of finding employment opportunities aligned with your skills, interests, and career goals. Graphic design is a diverse field with a wide range of career paths and opportunities for professionals with creative talents and visual communication skills.

Here are some strategies to consider as you explore your career paths:

Build a Strong Portfolio: Your portfolio is your most important tool for showcasing your skills and experience to potential employers. Select your best work that demonstrates your range, creativity, and proficiency in graphic design. Include a variety of projects, such as branding materials, print designs, digital graphics, and any other relevant work that highlights your abilities.

Network: Networking is crucial for finding job opportunities and building relationships within the industry. Attend networking events, workshops, conferences, and industry meetups to connect with other professionals, potential employers, and recruiters.

Utilize Online Job Boards: Explore online job boards and freelance platforms dedicated to creative professionals, such as *Behance, Dribbble, Creativepool,* and *Authentic Jobs*. Regularly search for graphic design job postings, filter by location, industry, and job type, and apply to positions that match your skills and interests.

Apply Directly to Companies: Research companies and organizations that you admire and are interested in working for. Visit their websites to see if they have any job openings for graphic designers or reach out directly to inquire about potential opportunities. Tailor your application materials, including your resume and portfolio, to demonstrate how your skills align with their needs.

Freelancing and Contract Work: Consider freelancing or taking on contract assignments as a way to gain experience, build your portfolio, and expand your network. Many companies and agencies hire freelance graphic designers for short-term projects or to assist with overflow work. Utilize freelance platforms like Upwork, Freelancer, and Fiverr to find freelance opportunities and projects.

Continuing Education and Skill Development: Stay current with industry trends, tools, and technologies by investing in ongoing education and skill development. Take online courses, attend workshops, and participate in webinars to learn new techniques, software applications, and design principles that can enhance your capabilities as a graphic designer.

Prepare for Interviews: Practice your interview skills and be prepared to discuss your design process, portfolio projects, and relevant experiences during job interviews. Research the company and the role you're applying for, and be ready to demonstrate how your skills and expertise can contribute to their organization.

Exploring Career Paths

By following the strategies previously mentioned and actively engaging in the job market, you can increase your visibility, expand your professional network, and discover exciting opportunities as a graphic designer.

Consider the following strategies:

Connect with Professors and Instructors: Your professors and instructors from your graphic design program can serve as valuable mentors and sources of guidance. Reach out to them for advice, feedback on your work, and recommendations for industry connections. They may also provide insights into career paths, job opportunities, and resources for professional development.

Engage with Peers: Networking with fellow graphic design graduates can be mutually beneficial. Join professional groups, attend industry events, and seek out online communities where you can connect with peers. By sharing experiences, exchanging feedback, and collaborating on projects, you can stay motivated and learn from one another.

Leverage Industry Resources: Make the most of the resources available to you within the graphic design industry. Subscribe to design publications, follow influential designers and agencies on social media, and participate in relevant webinars and workshops. These resources will keep you updated on industry trends, provide inspiration, and offer valuable insights from experienced professionals.

Career Counselors: Seek advice from career counselors who can help you identify your interests, and guide you towards suitable career paths.

Professional Associations: Join professional associations like *AIGA* or *Graphic Artists Guild* for resources, mentorship programs, and career development opportunities.

Explore Different Specializations: Try working on projects in various specializations such as branding, web design, illustration, and motion graphics to discover what interests you the most.

Informational Interviews: Contact professionals working in roles you are interested in and request informational interviews. Inquire about their career journey, the skills required for their role, the challenges they face, and advice for someone starting in the field.

On the following pages, you will find an overview of career specializations in graphic design, including associated tasks and skills. Opportunities for specialization, growth, and advancement exist within each path, based on individual interests, skills, and career goals. There are overlaps in tasks and skills among UX/UI designers, digital web designers, motion graphics designers, and computer graphics designers. Each role involves design, creativity, and technical proficiency, but also has unique focuses and specialized skills. The shared tasks and skills highlight the interconnected nature of the design field. Understanding these overlaps and common threads can help professionals expand their skills and transition into other areas within the design industry. You can gain an understanding of the graphic design field, identify your interests, and make informed decisions about your career path.

Career Specializations

Graphic designers can find employment in a variety of industries and sectors. Additionally, increasing with those as user experience (UX) design, augmented reality (AR) design, and virtual reality (VR) design.

Some common types of jobs for graphic designers include:

The Print Designer:

Print designers specialize in creating visual materials for printed media, such as magazines, newspapers, books, brochures, posters, packaging, and more. They use their creativity and technical skills to design layouts, graphics, and typography that effectively convey information and communicate messages to a target audience.

Some of the tasks print designers engage in are:
- Designing Layouts
- Selecting Typography
- Creating Graphics
- Incorporating Branding
- Preparing Files for Printing
- Collaborating with Clients and Printers

Some of the skills print designers must have:
- Proficiency in Graphic Design Software
- Understanding of Typography
- Ability to Create Effective Layouts
- Knowledge of Color Theory
- Attention to Detail
- Effective Communication Skills
- Understanding of Print Production Processes

Overall, print designers need a combination of artistic creativity, technical proficiency, and attention to detail to create visually stunning and effective printed materials that meet the needs of clients and engage target audiences.

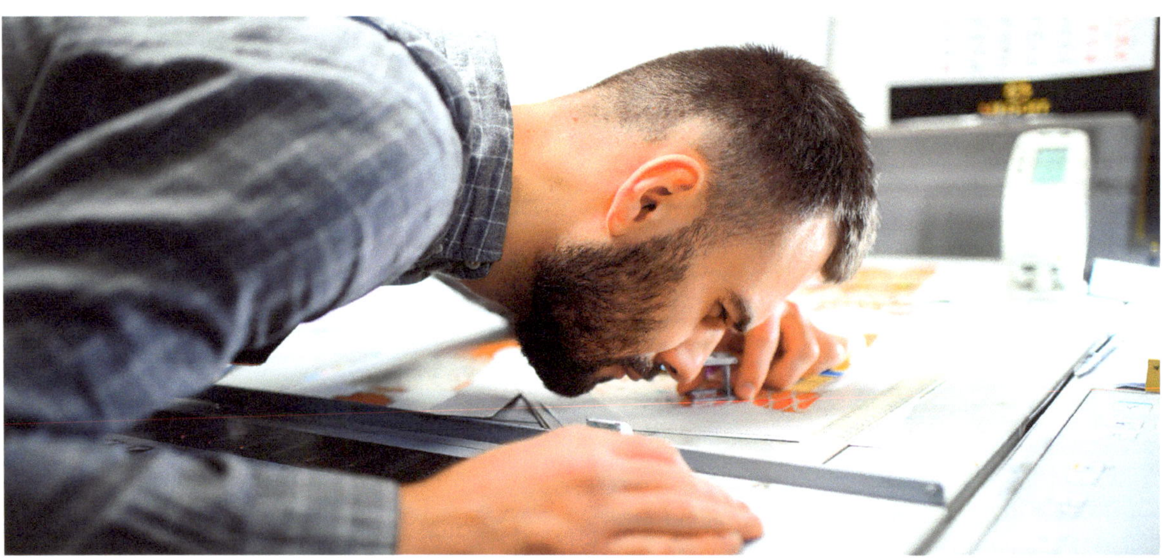

Print designer checking a print proof using a loupe to determine print color and image quality.

The Art Director:

An Art Director is a creative professional responsible for overseeing the visual aspects of a project or campaign and ensuring that they align with the overall creative vision and objectives. Art directors work across various industries, including advertising, marketing, publishing, film, television, and digital media. They collaborate with clients, creative teams, and other stakeholders to conceptualize and execute design solutions that meet project goals and requirements.

Some of the tasks associated with art direction:

- Creative Conceptualization
- Visual Development
- Mood Boards and Style Guides
- Art Direction
- Design Oversight
- Client Communication
- Project Management

Some of the skills associated with art direction:

- Creative Vision
- Leadership and Collaboration
- Communication and Presentation
- Strategic Thinking
- Problem-Solving Abilities
- Attention to Detail
- Industry Knowledge

Overall, an Art Director is a key creative role in various industries such as advertising, publishing, film, television, gaming, and digital media. They are responsible for overseeing the visual aspects of a project, ensuring that the artistic vision is executed effectively and aligns with the project's objectives and target audience. They shape the visual identity and creative direction of all projects, from conceptualization to execution.

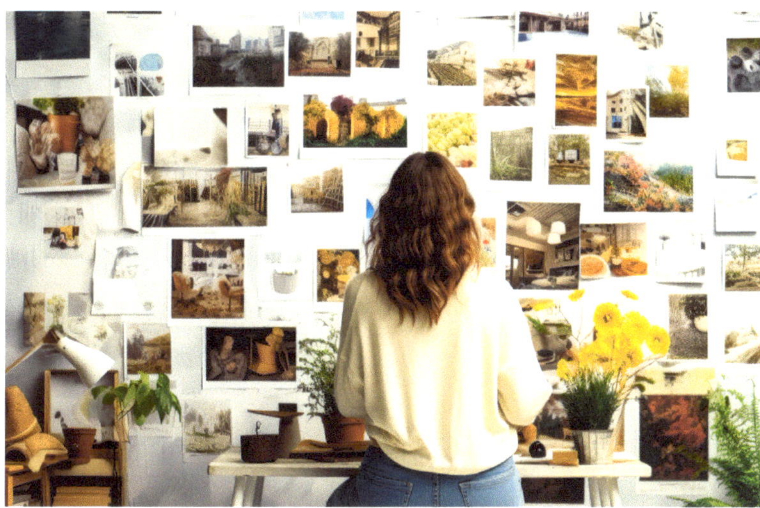

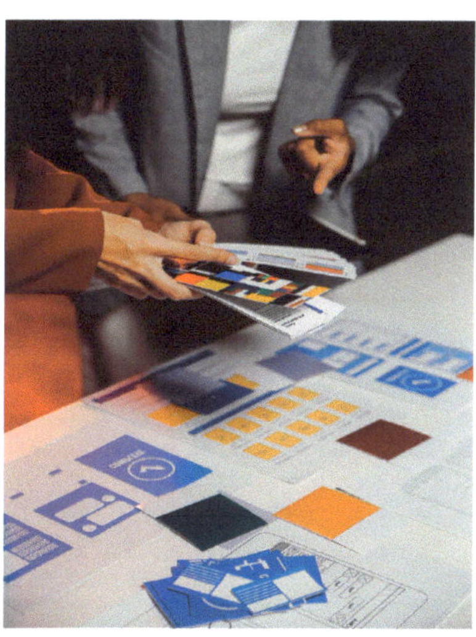

Left: *Art director contemplating a vision board.*
Right: *Art director collaborating with designer on colors for possible style guide.*

The UI/UX Designer:

A UI/UX designer, often referred to as a user interface/user experience designer, specializes in creating intuitive, engaging, and user-friendly digital experiences for websites, mobile apps, and other digital platforms. They focus on understanding user needs, behaviors, and preferences to design interfaces and experiences that optimize usability and enhance user satisfaction.

Some of the tasks associated with UI/UX design:

- User Research
- Wireframing and Prototyping
- Information Architecture
- User Interface Design (UI)
- User Experience Design (UX)
- Visual Design
- Accessibility
- Responsive Design
- Usability Testing
- Collaboration with Developers

Some of the skills associated with UI/UX design:

- User-Centered Design
- Proficiency in Graphic Design Software
- Familiarity with Prototyping Tools
- Knowledge of UX/UI Design Principles
- Having Problem-Solving Skills
- Communication and Collaboration
- Adaptability and Continuous Learning

Overall, UI/UX designers play a critical role in creating digital products that are intuitive, engaging, and enjoyable to use, ultimately enhancing the overall user experience and driving business success. They are essential in crafting digital experiences that meet user needs and drive business goals.

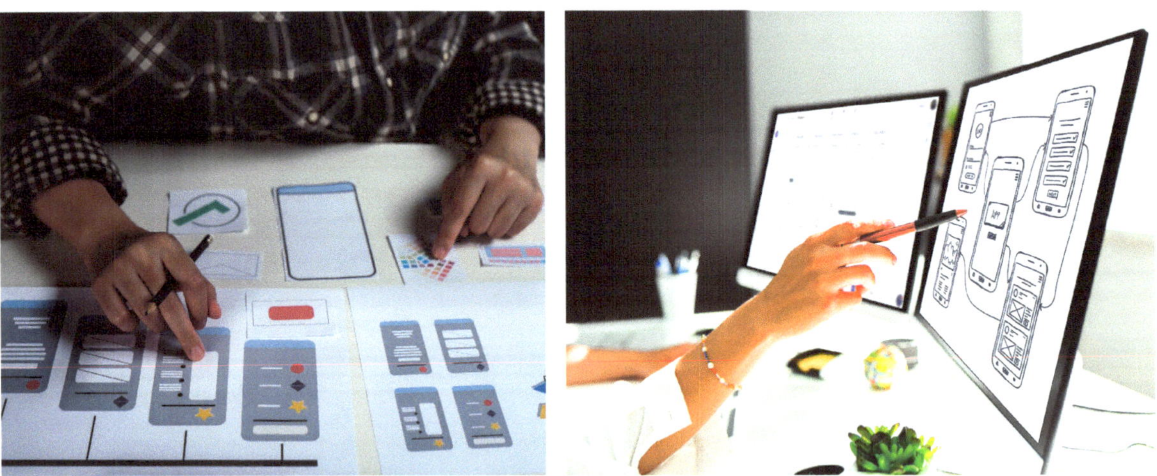

UI/UX Designers at work engaging in wireframing, prototyping, and visual problem-solving

Digital/Web Designer:

Digital or web designers specialize in creating visual designs for digital platforms, including websites, mobile apps, social media graphics, email campaigns, and online advertisements. They may work closely with web developers to ensure that designs are optimized for user experience and functionality across various devices and screen sizes.

Some of the tasks associated with digital web design:

- Designing User Interfaces (UI)
- Crafting User Experience (UX)
- Creating Wireframes and Prototypes
- Selecting Visual Elements
- Incorporating Responsive Design
- Collaborating with Developers

Some of the skills a digital web designer must have:

- Proficiency in Design Software
- SEO and Web Analytics
- Responsive Design
- Interaction Design
- Project Management
- Problem-Solving
- Maintenance and Updates
- Collaboration and Communication

Overall, digital web designers require a blend of artistic creativity, technical proficiency, and user-centered design skills to produce captivating and successful digital experiences that satisfy the requirements of both clients and users.

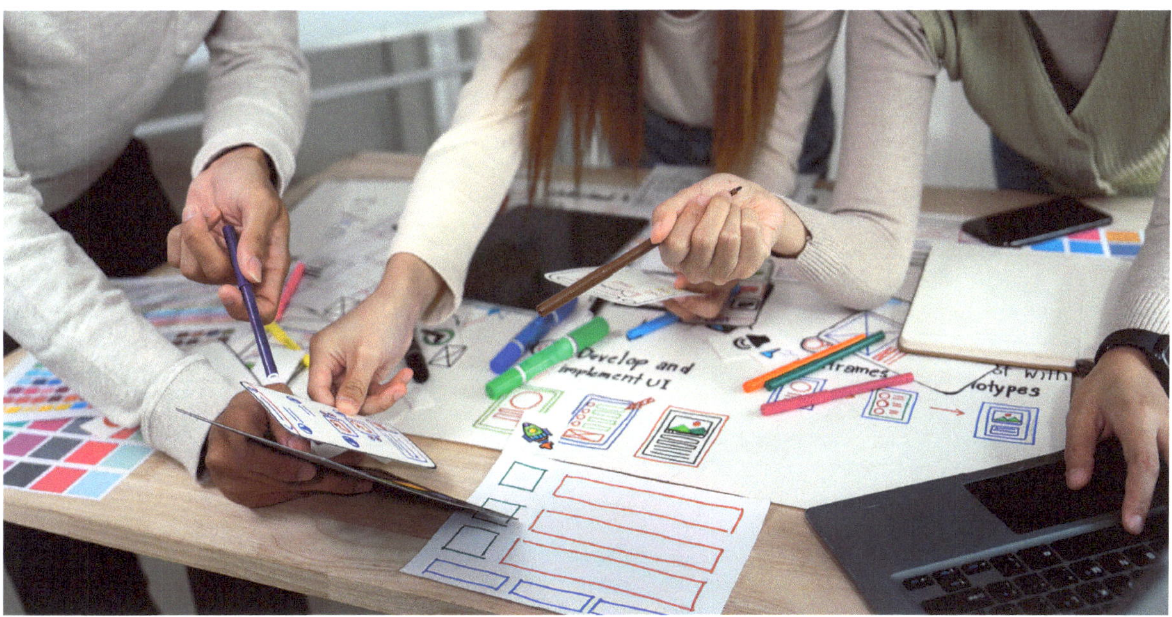

Digital web designers collaborating, evaluating, and problem-solving visual elements for mobile devices.

The Motion Graphics Designer:

Motion graphics designers blend graphic design and animation with visual effects to produce captivating motion graphics for film, TV, video games, and digital media. They employ animation software and video editing tools to infuse motion and storytelling into static designs. A Motion Graphics Designer is a creative expert specializing in crafting animated visuals for diverse media platforms, such as film, TV, advertising, and digital media. Employing animation, typography, and visual effects, they effectively communicate messages, tell stories, and captivate audiences.

Some of the tasks associated with motion graphics design:

- Concept Development
- Storyboarding
- Drawing skills
- Animation Design
- Visual Effects
- Audio Integration
- Editing and Post-Production
- Client Collaboration

Some of the skills associated with motion graphics design:

- Animation Software Proficiency:
- Graphic Design Skills:
- Storytelling Abilities:
- Motion Design Principles:
- Audio-Visual Integration:
- Creativity and Innovation:
- Attention to Detail:
- Collaboration and Communication:

Overall, motion graphics designers play a vital role in creating visually stunning and engaging animations that captivate audiences and communicate messages effectively across various media platforms. They combine artistic creativity, technical proficiency, and storytelling skills to produce compelling motion graphic content that leaves a lasting impression on viewers.

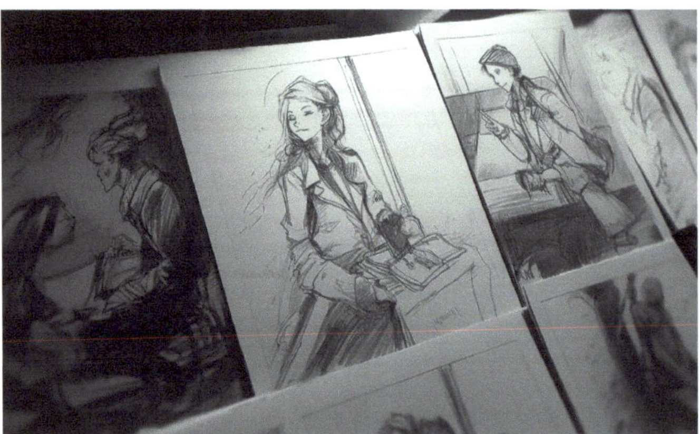

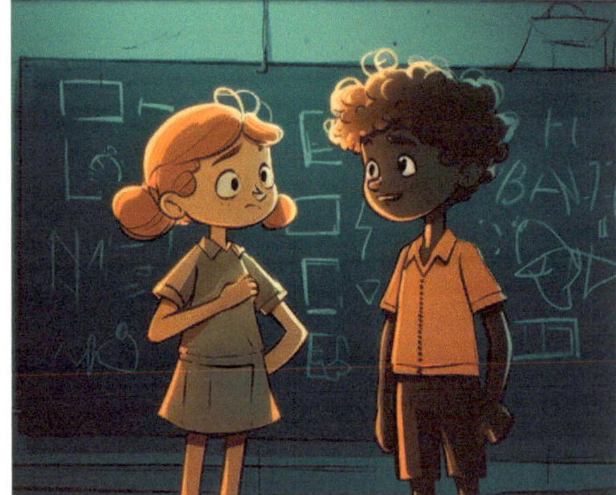

Left: *Pencil sketch storyboard for possible animation*
Right: *Characters of boy and girl digitally rendered for animation*

The Computer Graphic Designer:

Computer graphic designers use computer software and technology for creating and manipulating visual elements for design purposes. This encompasses various digital media creation forms, including digital illustration, photo editing, 3D modeling, animation, web design, and more. Specialized software like Adobe Creative Suite (e.g., Photoshop, Illustrator, InDesign), Autodesk Maya, or Blender is often used in computer graphic design to create and edit visual content.

Some of the tasks associated with computer graphics design:

- Creating Digital Illustrations
- Photo Editing and Retouching
- Designing Logos and Branding
- Layout Design
- Web Design
- 3D Modeling and Animation
- Typography
- Motion Graphics
- User Interface (UI) Design
- Collaborating with Clients and Team Members

Some of the skills required for computer graphic designers:

- Proficiency in Design Software:
- Creative Thinking and Problem-Solving
- Visual Communication Skills
- Attention to Detail
- Technical Skills
- Time Management and Organization
- Collaboration and Communication
- Adaptability and Learning Agility

In essence, computer graphic design is a subset of graphic design that focuses on digital tools and technologies for creating visual communication. While traditional graphic design methods may involve hand-drawing, painting, or collage techniques, computer graphic design leverages the capabilities of digital tools to produce professional-quality designs efficiently and effectively.

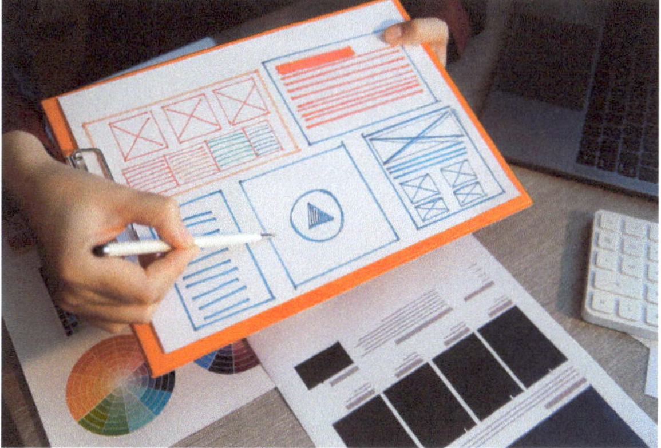

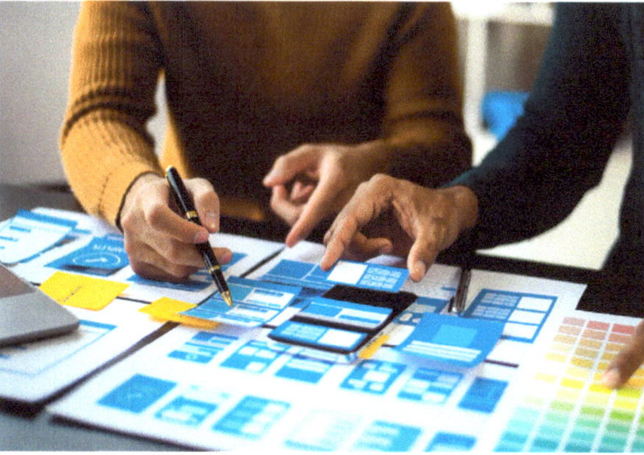

Computer Graphic Designers engaging in creative thinking and problem-solving

The Packaging Designer:

A packaging designer is a professional who specializes in creating the visual and structural design for product packaging. Their role is to create packaging solutions that not only protect and contain the product but also communicate the brand identity, attract consumers, and differentiate the product from competitors on the shelf. They consider factors such as branding, product visibility, shelf appeal, and regulatory requirements to create packaging solutions that are both functional and visually appealing packaging solutions. Packaging design for products include boxes, bottles, labels, and containers.

Some of the tasks associated with packaging design:

- Concept Development
- Creating compelling comps
- Structural Design
- Graphic Design
- Brand Integration
- Regulatory Compliance
- Production Coordination
- Consumer Testing

Some of the skills required for packaging design:

- Graphic Design Software Proficiency
- 3D Modeling Software Skills
- Structural Design Knowledge
- Creativity and Innovation
- Attention to Detail
- Communication Skills
- Problem-Solving Abilities
- Attention to Detail
- Marketing Knowledge

A comp (short for "comprehensive") in graphic design is a presentation of a structured visual that a graphic artist or advertising agency shows to a client. The purpose of the comp is to demonstrate the relative size and position of images and text, even if the client's specific images and text are not yet available.

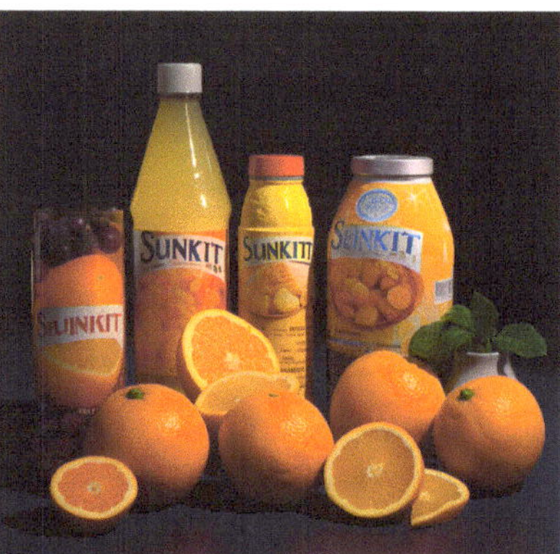

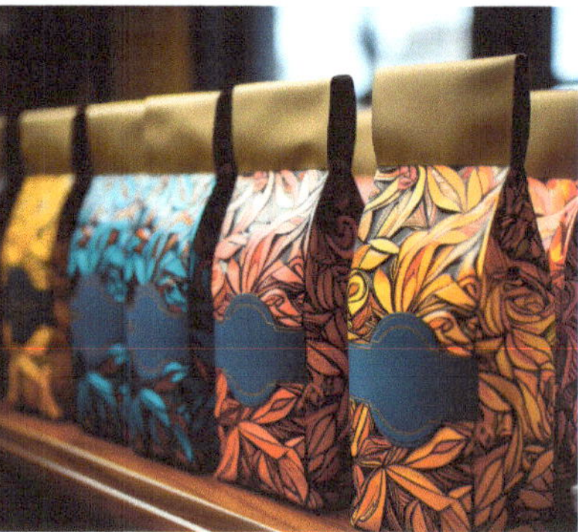

Above: *Box packaging design template for possible beauty or lotion product with 3D box mockup.*
Right: *Comps of juice bottle labels and comps of colorful coffee packaging.*

The Advertising Designer:

An advertising designer is a creative professional who specializes in conceptualizing and creating visual elements for advertising campaigns across various media channels, including print, digital, outdoor, television, and social media. They collaborate with copywriters, art directors, and marketing teams to effectively communicate messages and engage target audiences. Their primary goal is to effectively communicate a brand's message or product offering to engage a target audience.

Some of the tasks associated with advertising design:

- Concept Development
- Visual Design
- Layout Design
- Brand Integration
- Copywriting Collaboration
- Adaptability Across Platforms
- Campaign Management

Some of the skills required of an advertising designer:

- Graphic Design Software Proficiency
- Creative Thinking
- Typography and Layout Design
- Brand Awareness
- Communication Skills

Overall, advertising designers play a crucial role in creating visually compelling and effective advertising materials that help brands stand out in a crowded marketplace and drive success for their advertising campaigns. They combine creativity, technical skills, and marketing knowledge to produce impactful designs that resonate with audiences and achieve business objectives.

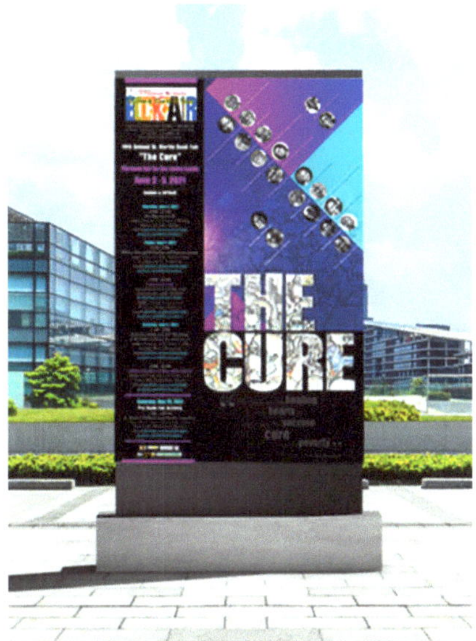

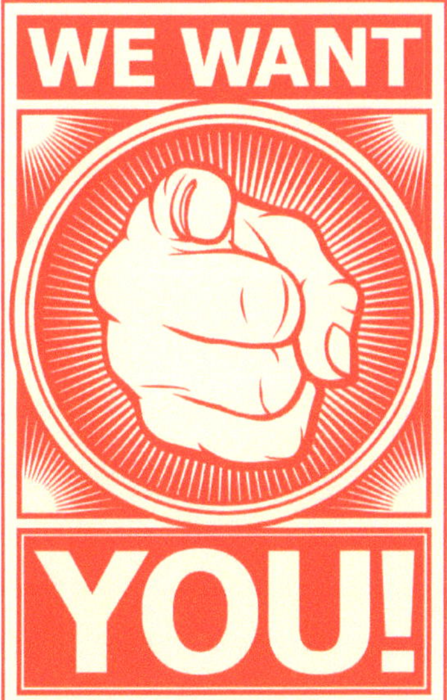

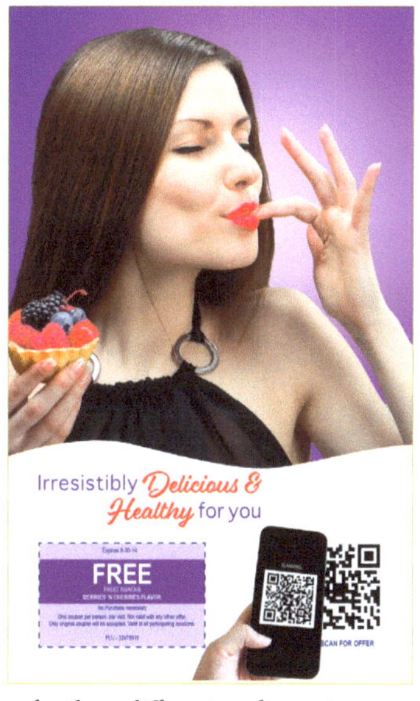

Mockups of three compelling ads for promotional purposes created by advertising designers for three different audience types.

The Brand Identity Designer:

A Brand Identity Designer specializes in creating visual elements that represent a brand's identity and communicate its values, personality, and messaging to its target audience. They work to develop cohesive and memorable brand identities that differentiate a company or product from its competitors and resonate with its audience.

Some of the tasks associated with Brand Identity Design:

- Brand Research
- Logo Design
- Visual Identity Development
- Brand Guidelines Creation
- Collateral Design
- Brand Application
- Client Collaboration

Some of the skills required for a brand identity designer:

- Graphic Design Software Proficiency
- Creative Thinking
- Brand Strategy
- Typography and Color Theory
- Communication Skills
- Attention to Detail
- Adaptability and Collaboration

Overall, Brand Identity Designers play a crucial role in shaping the visual identity of brands and creating cohesive and memorable brand experiences for customers. They combine creativity, strategic thinking, and design skills to develop brand identities that resonate with audiences and drive brand recognition and loyalty.

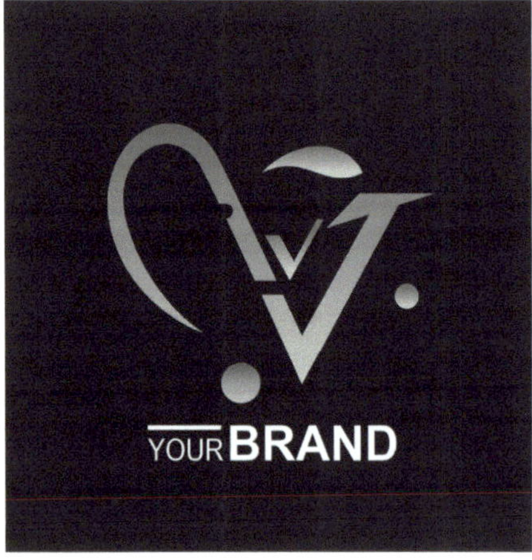

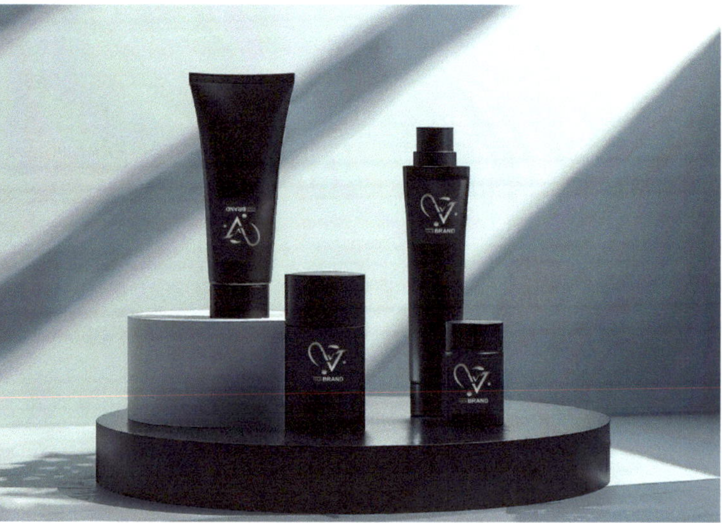

Above: *Logo, Brand Mark or Brand Identity*
Right: *Brand identity applied to company products.*

The Freelance Designer:

Freelance designers work independently or as contractors, providing design services to clients on a project-by-project basis. They have the flexibility to choose their own projects, clients, and work schedule, but also need to manage their own business operations, including client communication, project management, and invoicing. Freelancers work independently rather than being employed by a single company or organization.

However, although freelancing can sometimes be isolating, many freelancers find ways to stay connected through collaboration, co-working spaces, online communities, client interactions, and professional events. By actively seeking opportunities for connection and engagement, freelancers can enjoy a fulfilling and socially enriched design career.

An overview of some of the tasks associated with freelancing:

- Client Acquisition
- Project Management
- Service Delivery
- Client Communication
- Billing and Invoicing

An overview of some of the skills freelancers require:

- Technical Skills:
- Communication Skills
- Time Management
- Self-Motivation
- Business and Marketing Skills
- Problem-Solving Abilities
- Financial Management

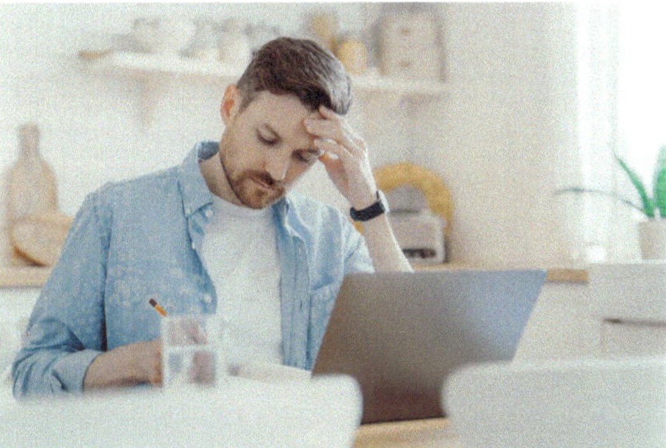

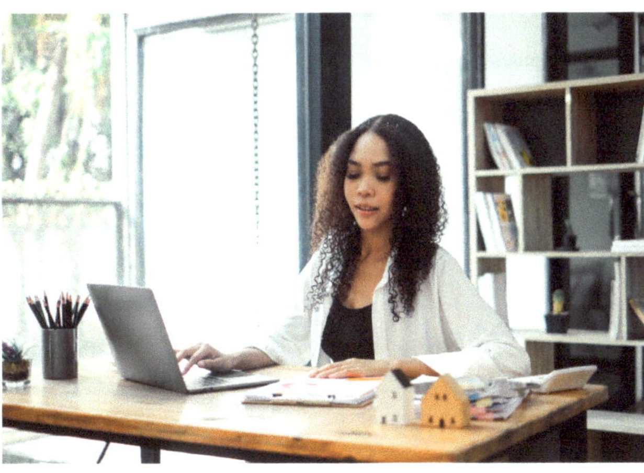

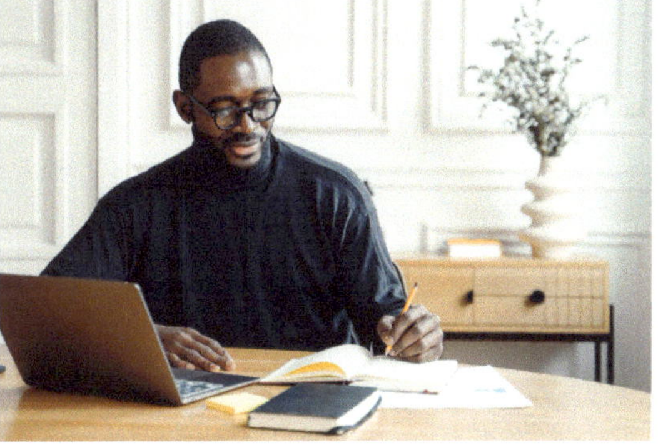

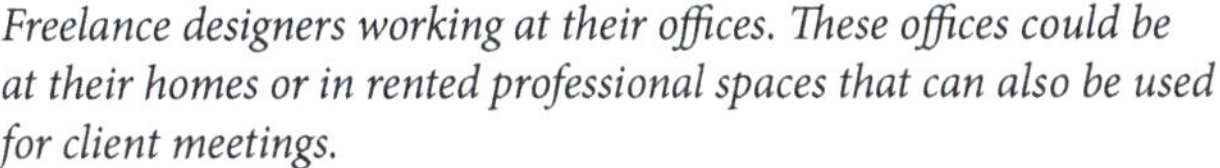

Freelance designers working at their offices. These offices could be at their homes or in rented professional spaces that can also be used for client meetings.

The Illustrator:

Illustrators occupy a unique niche within the broader field of graphic design. While graphic designers often focus on creating visual content that combines text and images to communicate messages effectively, illustrators specialize in creating original artwork. This artwork can be used in various contexts, including editorial content, advertising, product packaging, and more.

Some of the tasks performed by an illustrator:

- Creating Original Artwork
- Concept Development
- Storyboarding
- Attention to Detail
- Revisions and Edits
- Collaboration
- Research
- Portfolio Development

Some of the skills associated with illustration:

- Artistic Ability
- Creativity
- Technical Proficiency
- Attention to Detail
- Visual Storytelling
- Adaptability
- Communication Skills

Overall, illustrators play a crucial role and bring a unique set of skills to the graphic design field, focusing on the creation of original artwork that can stand alone or complement other design elements. Their ability to create visually engaging and narrative-driven images makes them indispensable in many creative industries.

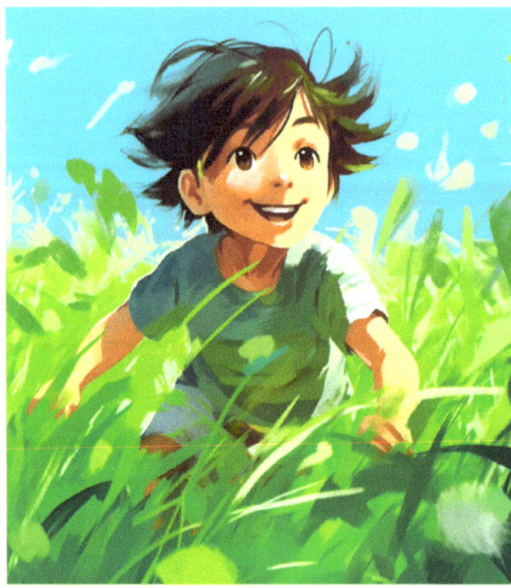

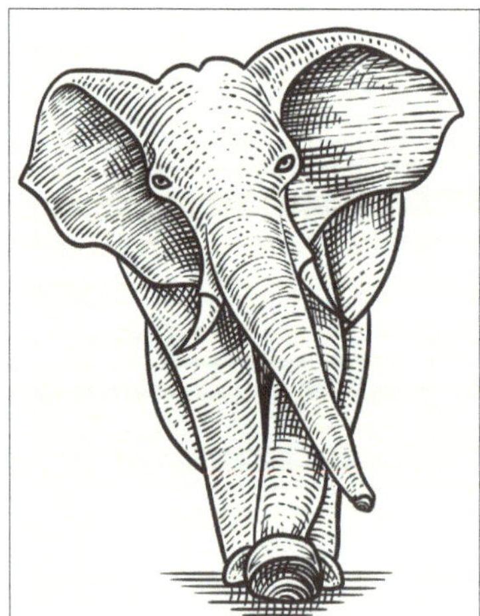

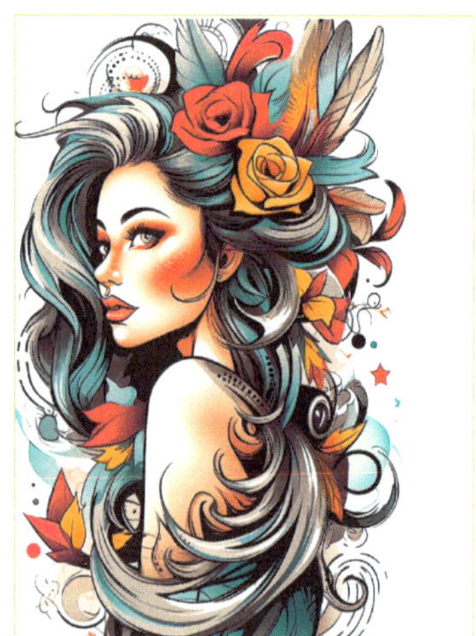

Some illustrators develop a unique and distinctive style much sought after by ad agencies, authors and and art galleries.

Where Can Graphic Designers Apply For Jobs?

Graphic designers have the opportunity to find employment in various industries and sectors. To ensure a good fit, it is crucial for them to research these industries and gain a comprehensive understanding of their operations. When seeking employment, graphic designers can choose to apply directly to the company, collaborate with a recruiter, or respond to a job posting.

Here are some common sectors and job types for graphic designers:

1. **Advertising agencies:** Graphic designers in advertising agencies are responsible for creating visual concepts and designs for advertisements, marketing campaigns, and promotional materials.

2. **Corporate design departments:** Many large companies have their own in-house design teams that handle the creation of branding materials, product packaging, presentations, and internal communications.

3. **Publishing houses:** Graphic designers working for publishing houses focus on designing book covers, layouts, and illustrations for books, magazines, newspapers, and digital publications.

4. **Freelance work:** Some graphic designers choose to work independently as freelancers, taking on projects from a variety of clients that range from small businesses to corporations.

5. **Marketing firms:** Graphic designers employed by marketing firms create visual content for digital marketing campaigns, social media, email newsletters, and other promotional materials.

6. **Web design companies:** Graphic designers with expertise in web design specialize in creating user interfaces, website layouts, and graphics for websites and web applications.

7. **Film and television industry:** Graphic designers in the entertainment industry are responsible for designing motion graphics, title sequences, and visual effects for films, television shows, and online video content.

8. **Gaming industry:** Graphic designers within the gaming industry focus on creating artwork, user interfaces, characters, and environments for video games and mobile games.

9. **Education:** Some graphic designers work in educational institutions, where they design educational materials, textbooks, visual aids, and multimedia presentations for teachers and students.

10. **Nonprofit organizations:** Graphic designers may also find opportunities in nonprofit organizations, where they create visual materials for fundraising campaigns, awareness initiatives, and advocacy efforts.

These are just a few examples, as there are numerous other potential job opportunities for graphic designers across various industries and sectors. Moreover, with the growing demand for user experience (UX) design, augmented reality (AR) design, and virtual reality (VR) design, the field of graphic design offers even more diverse possibilities. (Visit the Special Section).

CHAPTER FOUR (Special Section)
WHAT JOB IS RIGHT FOR **ME?**

How do I decide the right position and work environment for *me*?

A Special Section by Linda L. McCulloch, Contributing Author

Corporate In-House or Institutional In-House? Design Firm? Marketing/ Advertising Agency? Freelance? Freelance-to-Full-time?

In this section, we explore various work options available for graphic designers in the job market. Not the *type* of work, but rather ***where*** to work. This includes corporate in-house positions, agency or design firm roles, freelance opportunities, and remote work. We offer a comparison of various work environments, both pro and con.

We offer tips on how to identify the best fit for your skills and ambitions, as well as guidance on knowing when to stay and when to move on.

Choosing the type of job that is the right fit for you is challenging but also exciting. If you don't have experience yet in any particular type of position, i.e. corporate in-house vs. agency or design studio, freelance vs. full-time, etc. then leave your options wide open. Remember, this will be the starting point for your graphic design career, and limiting your options before you have more experience could result in you missing out on that first great opportunity.

A NOTE ABOUT INDUSTRIES AND COMPANY CULTURE

Traditional Corporations: Many traditional corporate environments, such as finance, human resources, and administration, typically adhere to regular hours with minimal overtime, and allow for work-life balance.

Tech and Startups: In contrast, tech companies and startups might expect more overtime due to fast-paced development cycles and product launches.

ROLES AND RESPONSIBILITIES:

Executive and Managerial Positions: Higher-level positions might require more overtime, especially during critical business periods like end-of-quarter reporting, product launches, mergers or acquisitions.

Support Roles: Roles in Web design, UX/UI design, customer support, IT support, or other functions that require round-the-clock availability might also demand more overtime.

GEOGRAPHIC AND LEGAL CONSIDERATIONS:

Location: Overtime expectations can vary by country due to different labor laws and cultural attitudes towards work. For example, countries with strong labor protections (like many in Europe) tend to have lower overtime expectations.

Legal Framework: In some places, labor laws restrict the amount of overtime and mandate additional pay, which can influence company policies to limit overtime hours.

REMOTE WORK AND FLEXIBILITY:

The rise of remote work and flexible scheduling has changed the landscape for many corporate in-house jobs, allowing employees to balance their work hours more effectively and potentially reducing the need for overtime.

So! What types of positions are available for graphic designers for when first starting out?

- Corporate or in-house graphic design
- Advertising/Marketing Agency or Design Studio (includes motion graphics, Web design, UX/UI design, gaming design, etc.)
- Freelance Work: Remote, In-House or both
- Contract Work: Short and Long-Term

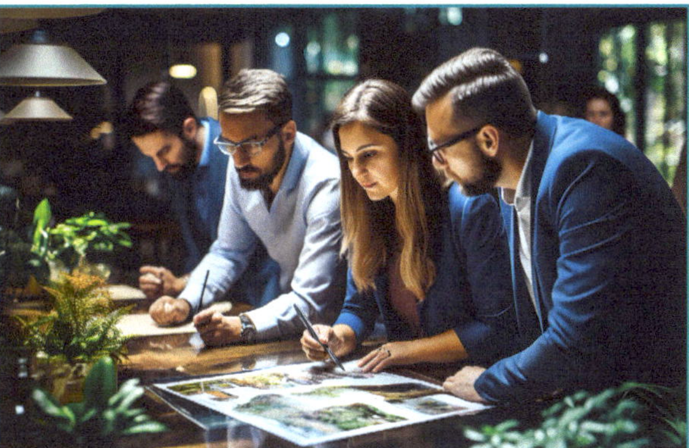

In-house designers can quickly make changes and create and distribute new content.

CORPORATE OR INSTITUTIONAL IN-HOUSE GRAPHIC DESIGN

Many large companies and some smaller ones find it more economical and efficient to have designers in-house. The company has the resources right at hand to create and distribute new or updated content quickly. Plus, they usually have a strict set of brand guidelines, ensuring that the work produced is accurate from the start and requires fewer revisions.

What are the advantages and disadvantages for you, the designer?

WHAT REAL WORLD DESIGNERS SAY:

"I never wanted to freelance and have to deal with finding clients and all the billing and so on. My job with a university in their creative department allows for great work-life balance and I get to do good work, so feel like I'm where I'm meant to be... for now."

Jill Carson, Winston Salem
Director of Design and Print Production
Large university

THE ADVANTAGES (In-House)

SALARY

You get a regular salary, plus benefits, usually after a three to six-month probationary period.

BENEFITS

Benefits can include:

- Health insurance.
- Vacation time (after a certain period of employment).
- Comp or compensation time (additional paid time off – PTO– for extra hours or weekends).
- Paid sick leave, paid maternity/paternity leave.

HOURS

- Most corporate in house jobs do not require a lot of overtime.
- Many corporate in-house jobs maintain a 40-hour workweek with minimal overtime.

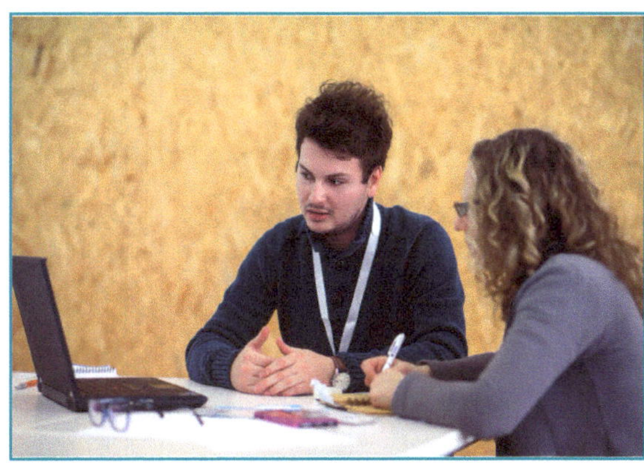

Performance reviews will help you and your employer identify your strengths and weaknesses

ADVANCEMENT

- Performance reviews will help you and the employer identify your strengths, weaknesses, successes, and areas for improvement.
- If the company is well known, you can acquire some valuable portfolio work to help you in your career progression.

THE DISADVANTAGES (In-House)

SALARY

May be much lower initially than you like or feel like you "deserve." Make sure it is enough to cover your expenses and inquire about the possibility of a performance review in a few months with the potential for a raise if the review is excellent.

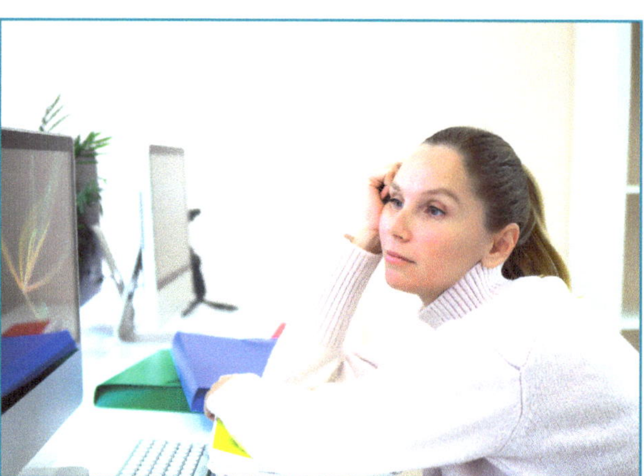

Working in an in-house corporate environment and doing design work for only one kind of product or service can lead to boredom and dissatisfaction.

BENEFITS

Benefits may not include, or may be less than desirable:

- Health insurance (not all employers cover it, or only cover a percentage).
- Vacation time, after a certain period of employment, may be limited to only a week per year.
- There may be no comp or compensation time. (additional paid time off – PTO– for extra hours or weekends).
- There may be little or no paid sick leave, little or no paid maternity/paternity leave.

HOURS

Overtime may be required for a new product launch, trade show or other deadline. Comp time or additional time may not be offered.

- Try to find out about the expected work hours in advance but avoid asking during the initial interview stage.

ADVANCEMENT

In this type of position, a designer will normally work on one type of design related to the company's products or services. This can lead to:

- Boredom.
- Dissatisfaction.
- Lack of creativity.

However, if the work is interesting and creative enough, it can still provide a steppingstone to your next great job!

> *For many new designers, working in a corporate or in-house institutional environment is a great start due to stable work hours and dependable work, which provide an excellent foundation for furthering their careers.*

HIRING PROCESS and POLITICS

The hiring process can be complicated:

- Multiple HR interviews.
- Psychological and other types of tests, including drug tests, background checks, even credit checks.

It can be intimidating and invasive, but again, if the job seems interesting and worthwhile, it may be worth agreeing to these additional requirements.

Office politics can be an issue:

- Most graphic designers are extremely competitive.
- It can feel like you are in a race rather than part of a team.
- Bad bosses can exacerbate these challenges.

ADVERTISING/MARKETING AGENCY OR DESIGN FIRM

There are some minor differences between an advertising/marketing agency and a design studio, but for purposes of this section we will address them together with a brief description of the differences.

A design firm or agency large enough to sustain designers and art directors allows for more room for advancement. And working on different accounts will expand a new designer's skills and portfolio.

Advertising/marketing agencies can handle large branding campaigns that can include social media, print, broadcast, outdoor, trade shows and much more. Although they may have some nonprofit clients, many of their clients are larger for-profit companies.

Design studios are usually, but not always smaller than agencies. They focus more on design than on advertising, and can still handle branding and publicity or awareness campaigns, but are not as involved in as many types of media as ad agencies. Motion graphics design firms come in many different forms, and much depends on exactly what kind of motion graphics are involved.

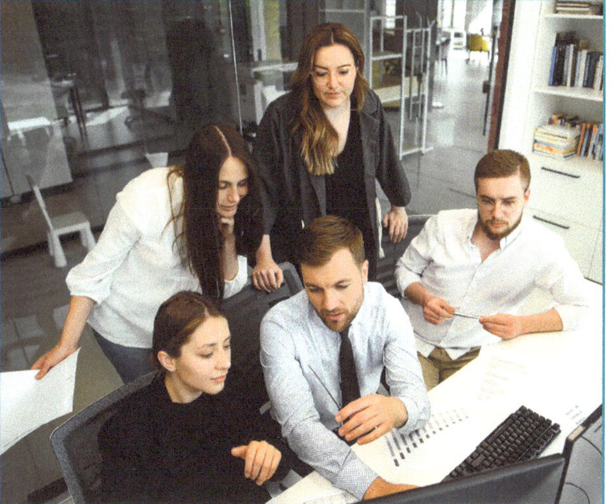

A team of designers and an art director discussing concepts and layouts for a marketing campaign

THE ADVANTAGES (Agency/Design Firm)

So! What are the advantages for you, the designer? What are the disadvantages?

Let's go with the advantages first, which can be similar to the Corporate In-House position.

SALARY

You get a regular salary, plus benefits, usually after a three to six-month probationary period.

BENEFITS

Benefits can include:

- Health insurance.
- Vacation time (after a certain period of employment).
- Comp or compensation time (additional paid time-off – PTO–for extra hours or weekends).
- Paid sick leave, paid maternity/paternity leave.

In-house corporate positions at a large company can require a lengthy hiring process, including psychological tests, background and even credit checks

THE ADVANTAGES (Agency/Design Firm, continued)

HOURS

Overtime may sometimes be required:

- Find this out in advance if possible, by asking questions about the kind of hours you are expected to work– but not in the initial interview stage!

Working in an agency or design firm can give a designer varied and creative experience, allowing for a more diverse portfolio with which to make their next great career move.

ADVANCEMENT

WHAT REAL WORLD DESIGNERS SAY:

"Out of college I knew I wanted to work in the agency world, so I did several internships and finally landed a really good job with a marketing agency, The Partnership. I started out as a Junior Designer and have worked my way up to a Junior Art Director role with more conceptual work. It was worth all the job searches and internships!"

Lindsay Muncy, Atlanta
Junior Art Director
Marketing and brand communications agency

- Performance reviews will help you and the employer identify your strengths, weaknesses, successes, and areas for improvement.
- There is usually room for advancement, particularly if the agency is large enough to sustain designers and art directors.
- Working on different accounts will expand your skills and your portfolio. You may start on a lower level on one account but as you prove yourself, you should be allowed to work on more diverse projects.

In a smaller company you may be required to perform many different tasks:

- Presenting to clients.
- Explaining the concepts and fundamental basics and strengths of your work.
- Pulling together estimates and quotes for projects.
- Answering phones, and even sending client emails.

This may not seem like the best use of your creative mind and talents, but it is invaluable experience that will benefit you greatly in the future.

If the company and/or its clients are well known, you will acquire some good portfolio work to help you move onward and upward.

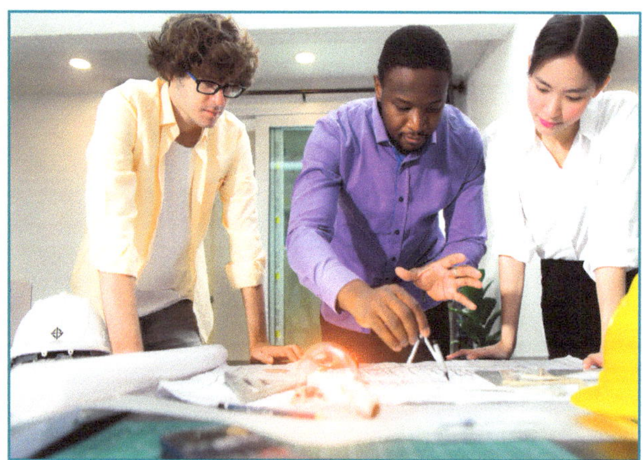

Agency art director and designers working closely together on a new product launch

HIRING PROCESS AND POLITICS

Small to medium firms may not require as much pre-screening:

- You may start out as a freelancer, with possible full-time later.
- Or you may need to provide your portfolio, credentials and references.

THE DISADVANTAGES (Agency/Design Firm)

SALARY

Salary is based on a 40-hour week, and includes benefits, similar to a corporate in-house position, but:

- Overtime is often required; it is advisable to find out in advance about the expected working hours if possible.
- Unpaid overtime is more common in a design or advertising firm.

BENEFITS

The benefits offered may include many of the same benefits as a corporate in-house position, but may not be as generous:

- Health insurance may cost less but offer less coverage.
- There may be fewer vacation days, even after a certain period of employment.
- No compensation or additional paid time off (PTO) for extra hours or weekends.
- May be less or no paid sick leave, paid maternity/paternity leave.

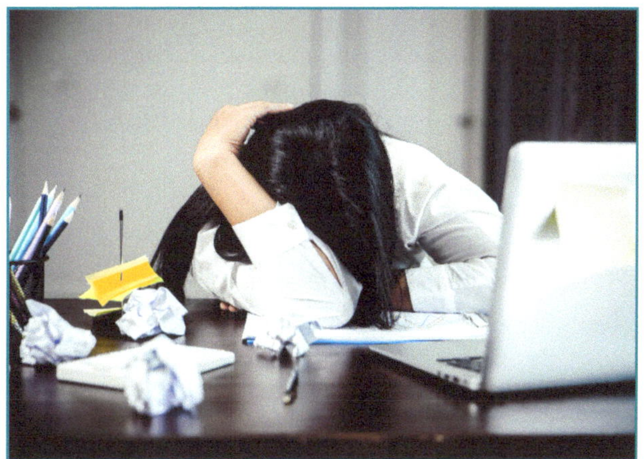

In a fast-paced and and very busy agency or design firm, overwork and burnout can become a problem, especially for a new designer.

HOURS

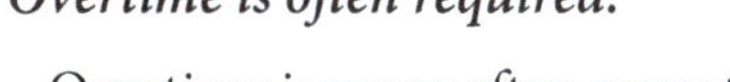

Overtime is often required:

- Overtime is more often expected and required in an agency or design firm than in corporate or in-house positions.
- There is frequently no compensation for overtime hours.
- Burnout from overwork can become a real problem.

ADVANCEMENT

- Performance reviews may be infrequent or nonexistent, depending on the company's size and leadership hierarchy.
- Advancement opportunities may be limited in small companies.

Additional tasks and roles may not align with your interests or strengths, for example:

- Presenting to clients.
- Explaining the concepts and strengths of your work.
- Providing estimates and quotes.
- Answering phones, sending emails, running errands, etc., may seem too boring or mundane to sustain your interest.
- The company's size or lack of reputation may not contribute to your career growth.

THE DISADVANTAGES (Agency/Design Firm, continued)

HIRING PROCESS AND POLITICS

- Many agency/marketing/design studio jobs are described in career opening posts as "fast-paced, lively, fun, collaborative" and other descriptive but vague phrases.
- *"Fast-paced"* and *"lively"* might actually mean working 60+ hours a week, but no compensation.
- Craft careful questions about these types of issues, once you are further into the interview phase.

Office politics can still be a concern:

- Most graphic designers are extremely competitive.
- It can feel like you are in a race rather than part of a team.
- Having a bad boss can exacerbate the situation.

If you have a bad boss, consider learning everything you can and move on.

FREELANCE WORK (REMOTE, IN-HOUSE, YOUR OWN CLIENTS, ETC.)
Including a special section for Short or Long-Term Contract Work

Freelance work is very different from working in a full-time, salaried job. But there are some similarities. You can still do corporate in-house work, design for an advertising/marketing agency, or work for a boutique design firm; or even all of these. And this can include both work on-site and remote work.

Freelance designers frequently have far more responsibilities than salaried designers in full-time positions. If you want to freelance full-time you will have more "freedom" than a salaried designer, but the "freedom" comes with some costs. Let's talk about the advantages first, since they're more fun!

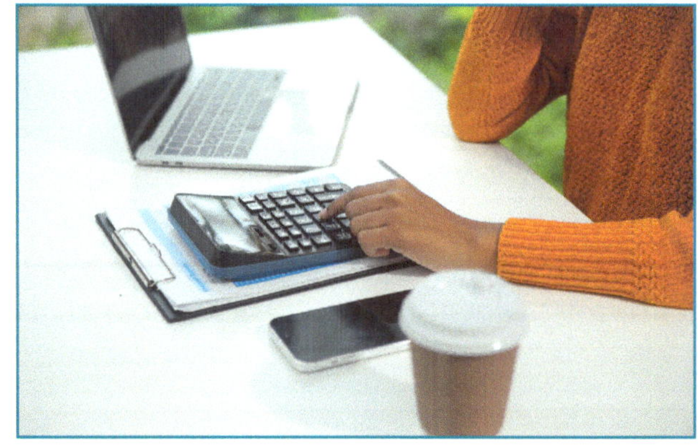

In a freelance career, you essentially determine your own salary by creating a budget of your expenses and then calculating what your income needs to be.

THE ADVANTAGES (Freelance Work)

SALARY

You "determine" your own salary. Essentially, you create a budget of your expenses and then calculate what your income needs to be. Starting out, this can be a challenge but as you gain experience you can raise your hourly rates and/or project fees.

BENEFITS

Freelancing allows for a wide range of experiences:

- Expand your network in many different ways.
- Working for different types of firms lets you discover, and narrow down, what kind of environment is best for you.

- You can acquire a larger and more diverse portfolio.
- You can acquire a larger and more varied range of clients.
- You may earn more respect from clients, especially if they are a small business, since you are being hired as an "outside expert."
- In an agency or design firm you may also be treated with more deference than the in-house creatives (although this can also be a disadvantage, as you will see in the next section).

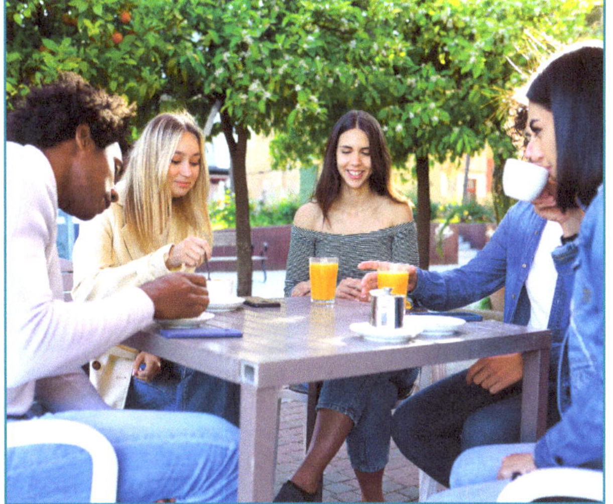

Freelance designers have more control over their work hours and can take time for lunch or coffee with a colleague

You are your own boss – up to a point:

- You can decide this work is not for you, and leave on good terms (never in the middle of a project!).
- You can decline work that you believe is not a good fit, or if the business or agency is representing something you find unattractive (such as political campaigns, for example).

NOTE: The client will always be your ultimate boss, whether that may be an in-house art director, creative director, marketing communications manager, or the end-user client.

HOURS

You have control over how many, or how few, hours you work:

- You can work extra hours for more pay (if you work at an hourly rate).
- You can also turn down work in order to achieve a better work-life balance.
- If the client or agency is too demanding and you have been clear about your availability, you can decline additional hours.

ADVANCEMENT

You will learn many different roles:

- Sales (pitching your services and showing your portfolio).
- Estimating budgets and getting approval, to best ways of invoicing the client to keep the revenue flowing.
- Presenting work to clients and effectively explaining the concepts, fundamental basics and strengths.
- Communicating with clients and others (team members, art directors etc.) in a professional, clear and pleasant manner.

WHAT REAL WORLD DESIGNERS SAY:

"My husband and I started out as freelancers and then formed our own small company. It worked for us for many years, and we had a great work life-balance, whether we were working for agencies or our own clients."

Janie Morgan, Stone Mountain
Co-owner, small design firm

Linda McCulloch's Note: CORPORATE CLIENT AFFLICTIONS *is one of my favorite series of strips by Hilary Price.*

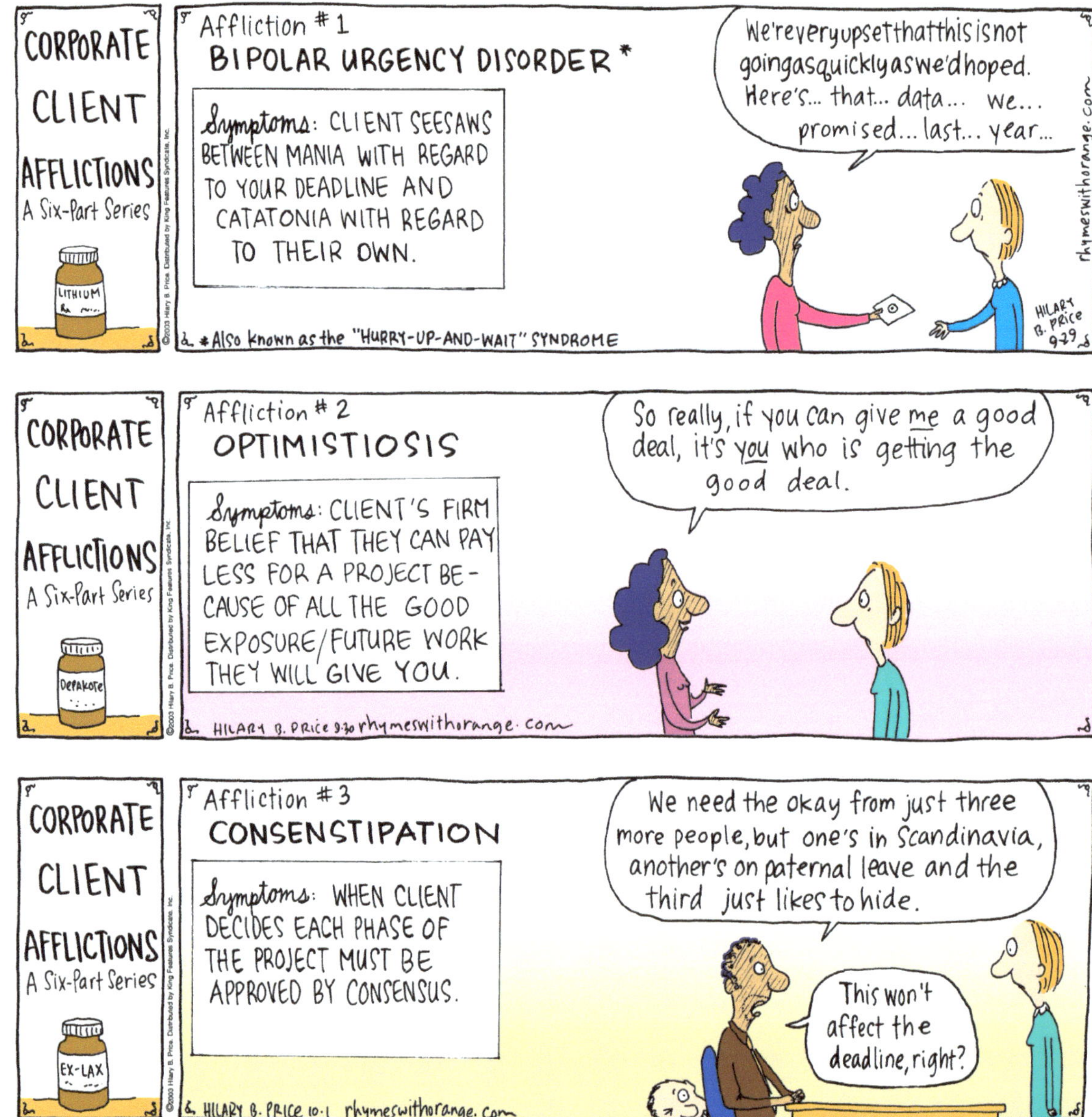

THE ADVANTAGES (Freelance Work, continued)

Once you have been successfully freelancing for a while, in agencies, design firms and/or in-house corporate environments, you can start to attract your own direct business clients.

"Direct" means you are working directly with the owner, marketing director or account/creative manager of the end-user client, rather than having the agency or design firm as an intermediary. If you prefer having fewer "layers" between you and the actual client, you can build up this business gradually, keeping the agency/design firm clients, until you establish your own small design firm. Although this requires a lot of work and time, it can also be incredibly rewarding.

Price's work illustrates the humor in many aspects of freelance work, but also refers to some of the issues faced by almost all graphic designers at some point in their careers. Laugh! It's good for you!

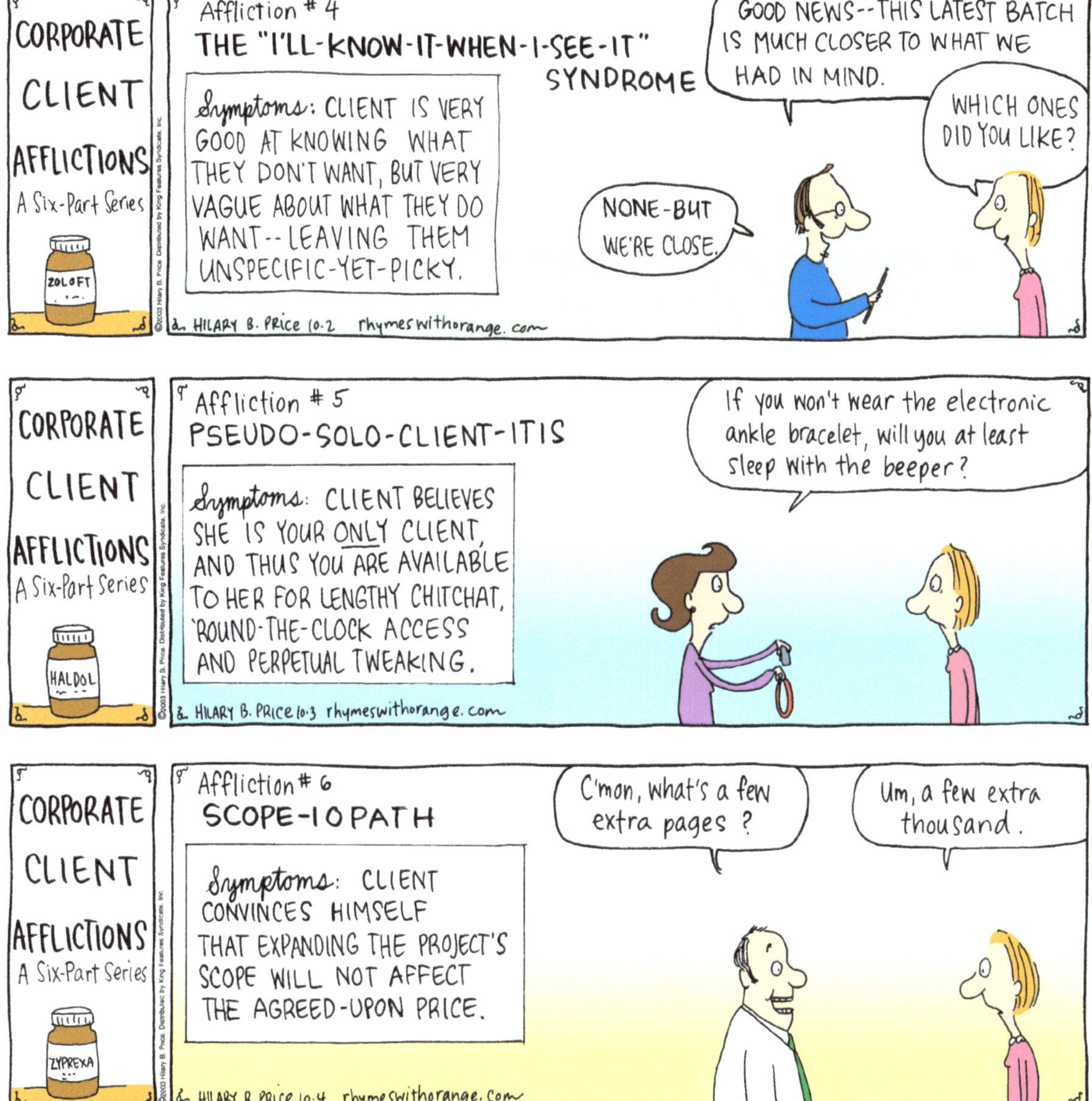

Rhymes With Orange © 2003 RWO Studios, Distributed by King Features Syndicate, Inc.

And you must be always networking, refining your sales pitch, and consistently impressing your clients. If you are naturally outgoing and like interacting with people, freelancing will be interesting and even fun.

HIRING PROCESS AND POLITICS

Offering your services as a freelancer is usually straightforward:

- Your portfolio, website and references are frequently all you need to secure the work or project.
- A short period of a day or so may be all that's needed above the interview and portfolio, to make sure you "mesh" with the team and/or client and can fulfill the expected work.

THE DISADVANTAGES (Freelance Work)

- Working as a freelancer for an agency or in-house creative department allows you to observe how they treat their full-time creatives. This insight can help your decision about accepting a full-time position if one is offered.
- As a freelancer, you can mostly avoid office politics since you are not a full-time employee.

SALARY

The lack of an actual salary can be a major issue:

- You have to charge affordable rates, yet still make a living.
- Tracking your hours is crucial to determine if you are charging enough per project – whether you are billing hourly or a flat fee for a specific project.
- Competition for freelance jobs is fierce. See the previous chapter for freelance websites you can join.
- You may find yourself bidding against others who are willing to underbid you significantly, resulting in either no work or inadequate pay.

The lack of benefits in a freelance career can be a real concern. Designers new to the freelance world should consult accountants and create budgets for health inusrance and other uncovered expenses.

THE DISADVANTAGES (Freelance Work, continued)

BENEFITS

There are no paid benefits.

- No health insurance.
- No vacation time.
- No sick leave, maternity or paternity leave.

Health insurance is critical. If you have a partner who is full-time, you can get on their plan, but you still will not have PTO (Paid Time Off). This frequently means that your time off is essentially time in which you have no billable work, so you must use your non-billable time wisely: updating your portfolio, your website, doing more networking, etc.

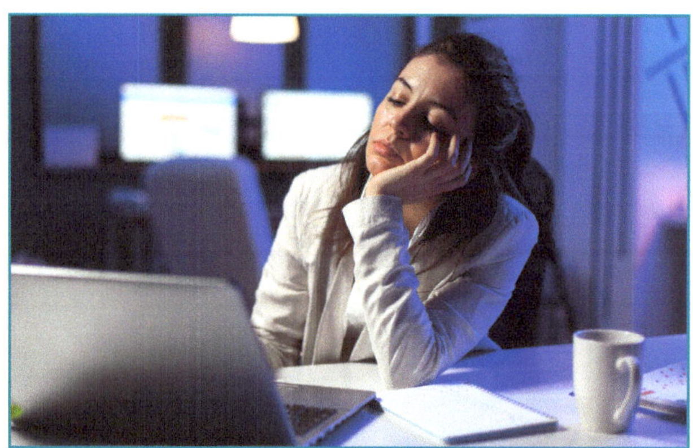

Freelancers must sometimes work long hours, resulting in exhaustion and lack of work-life balance.

Vacation time is determined by when you can afford it and still meet the work deadlines.

HOURS

Starting at an agency or design firm working remotely or in-house, you will be expected to work extra hours, sometimes many:

- Agencies and design firms frequently hire freelancers specifically for tight deadline or overflow work.
- The hours can be brutal, even if you are charging hourly. Establish the pay rate and your expected number of working hours in advance if possible.

Freelancers will have many roles, including sales, budgeting, billing, and presenting to clients, while still keeping their work fresh.

ADVANCEMENT

Your advancement is solely up to you:

- You will still be presenting work to clients such as art directors sales teams, etc.
- Explaining the concepts and fundamental basics of the work.
- Defending your work in a positive way.
- Networking, keeping your portfolio and your resumé fresh, etc.

You will have many roles:

- Sales (pitching your services and your portfolio).
- Estimating budgets and getting approval.
- Best methods of invoicing the client to keep the revenue flowing.

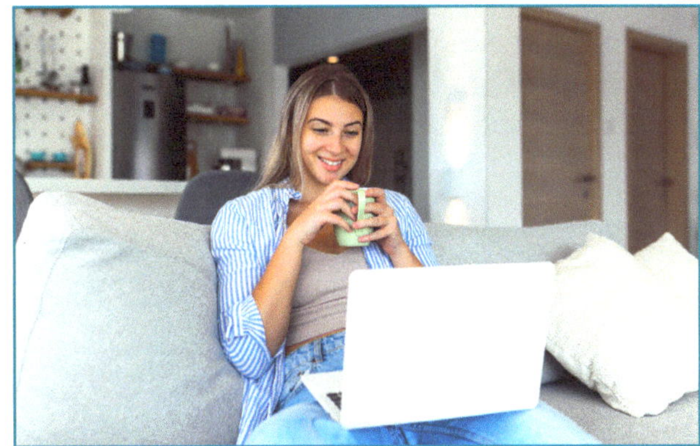

Freelance designers are responsible for their own advancement and many other responsibilities, but this can also be incredibly rewarding.

It's important to be aware that none of this is billable work. It's advisable to take some business classes targeted for designers and other creatives, and/or do a good bit of reading and research on best business practices, from sales to estimating to billing – and collecting, if you want to be a successful freelancer.

If you are not naturally outgoing, leaving the in-house agency/design firm world to strike out on your own and acquire your own clients may not be for you. This will become more clear to you as you advance in your career.

HIRING PROCESS AND POLITICS

The hiring process can be sketchy, if the agency/design firm is short-handed and needs someone to start right away:

- Your duties and work may not be clearly explained.
- You may find that you cannot get questions answered, or work reviewed, in a timely manner.
- Deadlines can be fluid or moved up arbitrarily.

Office politics can still be an issue:

- Paid full-time staff can be resentful of you, if they perceive that you have more freedom and are making "big bucks." This is a myth. "Big bucks" don't include you being responsible for health care, etc.

There can be blowback from the client/art director/account managers expecting you to skip important events or demand that you work whenever they say.

And "working whenever they say" is a myth also, since that is exactly the opposite of the definition of freelance.

WHAT REAL WORLD DESIGNERS SAY:

"Agency work can be interesting. It's never the same every day which I love. A certain challenge I have faced is, I've had four different Creative Directors in three years, but it's good to be a part of an agency that is growing and allowing me to do more of what I love: concept work, art directing, collaborating, presenting to clients, etc."

Lindsay Muncy, Atlanta
Junior Art Director
Marketing and brand communications agency

If you land in a bad freelance position or project, finish the work to the absolute best of your ability, learn everything you can and move on.

THE DISADVANTAGES (Freelance Work, continued)

TAXES (INCOME, SOCIAL SECURITY, ETC.)

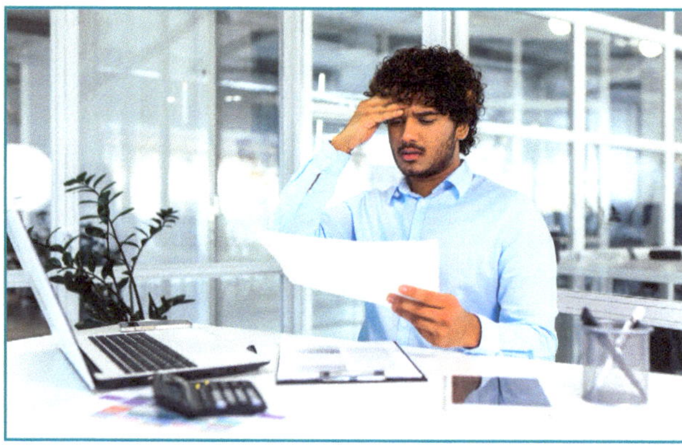

New freelancers have to contend with not having an actual salary, and be much more vigilant about their hourly rates and invoicing, as well as paying their bills on time.

You are responsible for your own tax withholdings, and this is CRITICAL, because it includes Social Security withholdings.

- As a self-employed person, you must pay **12.4% Social Security tax on up to $168,600 of your net earnings and a 2.9% Medicare tax on your entire net earnings.**
- Full-time W-2 employees pay half of their Social Security taxes and the employer pays the other half.
- You must withhold the above percentage from every check you get, after any out-of-pocket expenses for the project, plus a percentage for Federal Income Tax and State Income Tax.
- Some states, like Georgia, have State Income Tax, and some. like Florida, do not. It's highly advisable to consult an accountant about this before you have been freelancing for very long.
- If you nelect your quarterly tax payments, you will regret it when your income tax is due. The IRS, and your State Income Tax department (if your state has state income tax, see above paragraph) will charge you interest and penalties as well if you've not made your payments in advance.
- **NOTE: State Income Tax and Sales Tax are not the same.** State Income Tax (again, if your state has it) is based on your taxable income. Sales Tax is also administered by your State Revenue Department, but applies only to such tangibles you sell as part of your services, primarily printing.
- **It's advisable to avoid dealing with sales tax unless you are brokering large quantities of printing or other tangibles.** By then, you deserve to make a profit on these items. In that event it will be a good idea for you to invest in a bookkeeping/ accounting service or individual if you haven't already.

> *Freelancers are responsible for their own tax and Social Security withholdings. Consulting with an accountant is highly advisable.*

WHAT REAL WORLD DESIGNERS SAY:

> *"I didn't even negotiate my original salary, because I was freelancing, so anything looked good to me. I also wasn't aware that was an acceptable and commonplace thing to do. Don't be afraid to negotiate for a better starting salary, especially if you've already proved your worth to that company as a freelancer."*
>
> **Alaina Voerg, Atlanta**
> Executive Producer
> Corporate video company

FREELANCE WORK: SHORT/LONG-TERM CONTRACTS

Contract work, usually in the form of a six-month to one-year engagement for a specific project or job, involves several important considerations and can be considerably different from the type of work, etc. described in the previous freelance section. However, there can be some similarities, such as being responsible for your own tax and Social Security withholdings, for example. Ensure that you fully understand the terms of the contract and negotiate the best terms possible for yourself.

WHAT IS CONTRACT WORK?

Contract work is typically project-based and time-limited, meaning you are hired for a specific task or project for a set period, after which the contract ends unless renewed.

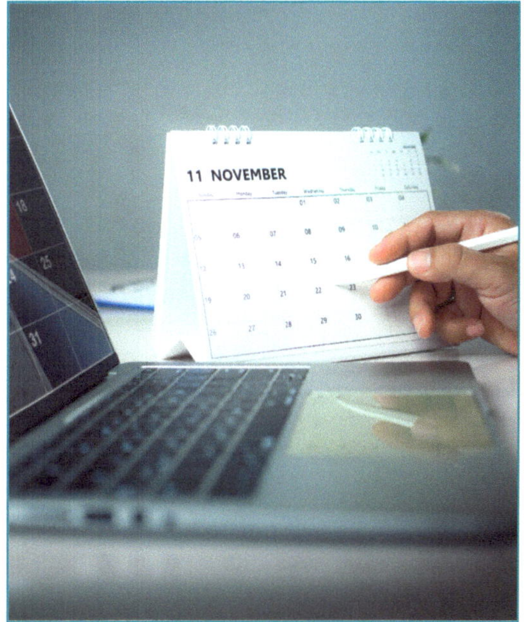

Contract work is usually a six-month to one-year period with fixed hours and rates.

CONTRACT TERMS AS TYPICALLY OUTLINED

Duration: The specific time frame of the contract (e.g., 6 months, 1 year).
Scope of Work: Detailed description of the tasks and responsibilities.
Compensation: Payment terms, which can be hourly, daily, weekly, or a fixed project fee.
Hours: Expected working hours, which may vary depending on the project needs.
Deliverables: Specific outputs or milestones that need to be achieved.

CONTRACT WORK HOURS AND OVERTIME

Flexibility: Contract workers often have flexible hours, but this depends on the nature of the project and the employer's requirements.
Overtime: It can vary depending on the project. Some contracts may include clauses about overtime pay, while others may expect completion within the agreed hours without additional compensation.

BENEFITS AND EMPLOYMENT STATUS

Benefits: Typically, contract workers do not receive benefits such as health insurance, retirement plans, or paid leave unless specified in the contract.

Employment Status: Contractors are often classified as independent contractors rather than employees, which affects eligibility for tax withholding and benefits.

LEGAL AND TAX IMPLICATIONS

Taxes: Contractors are usually responsible for their own taxes, including self-employment taxes (see TAXES in the Freelance section before this one).

Legal Rights: It is important to understand your rights under local labor laws, which frequently differ for contractors compared to full-time employees.

SHOULD I STAY OR SHOULD I GO? (When to stay and when to move on)

Whether you are working as a full-time designer or a freelance, in-house, remote, or contract, it's crucial to your career progress, your creative soul, and your sanity to know when to quit and/or move on. And it's equally crucial to know when to stay.

HERE ARE JUST A FEW SIGNS THAT IT'S TIME TO MOVE ON.

- The work is no longer challenging and/or creative and/or fun.
- Your original job description has changed, and not for the better (example: you were not hired to make sales calls and now you will be required to do that).
- The hours are brutal, and there is no work-life balance.
- Your superiors do not treat you well.
- You have not been given bigger and better projects as promised or expected, or received expected or promised promotions or monetary increases.
- There seem to be some internal issues with the company: payments are not arriving when expected; there have been one or more staff changes (and not for the better); gossip and/or nasty office politics are common; you are hearing unpleasant things about certain individuals.
- You are not being included in important concept sessions, presentations or meetings.

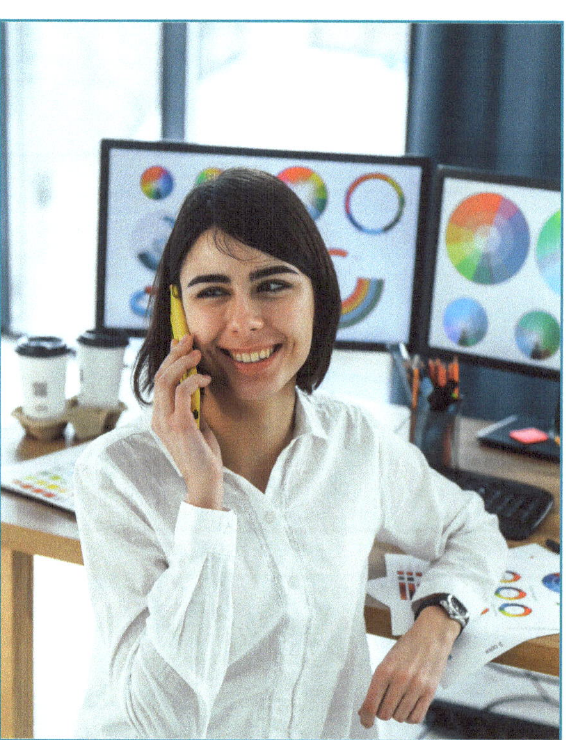

If the work is creative, the money is good and the people are nice, stay as long as possible!

SIGNS THAT YOU SHOULD STAY

- The work is creative, the money is good, and the people are nice (three out of three – dream job or client)!
- You are being challenged in good ways: bigger projects, more authority/responsibility and more respect.
- You and your colleagues/team members get paid on time, whether full-time or freelance.
- Your work is meaningful, the hours are reasonable, and your company or client respects your need for time off and a work-life balance.
- You feel seen and heard when you contribute to group discussions and teams.

WHAT REAL WORLD DESIGNERS SAY:

> *"If you have a client that respects your worth and your time, and pays you fairly, that client is worth working extra hard for, so you can keep them happy for longer."*
>
> **Janie Morgan, Stone Mountain**
> Co-owner, small design firm

A FUN EXERCISE

Using design as a metaphor, it becomes evident how various workplace environments can influence employee experience and productivity. A modern workplace, much like a masterpiece of modern design, is lively and inspiring, promoting creativity and collaboration. Conversely, a cluttered workplace, resembling a chaotic collage, overwhelms and distracts individuals, rendering it difficult to concentrate and perform their best. Furthermore, a dull workplace, comparable to a monochrome design, stifles imagination and drains enthusiasm and motivation, resulting in a lack of progress.

Would you consider creating a workspace that resembles a piece of modern art that can transform the way employees feel and perform, turning work into a source of inspiration and innovation?

Choose one of the designs below to determine where you would like to work as a new graduate. Then, engage in discussions with each other, sharing reasons why you selected a specific environment. Use the space beside each to jot down a few bullet points:

A

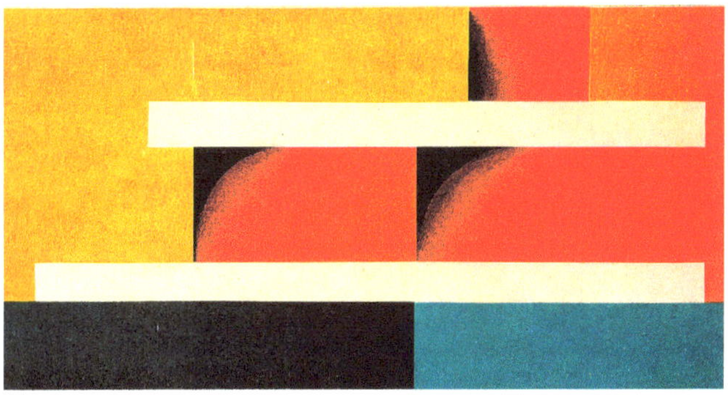

B

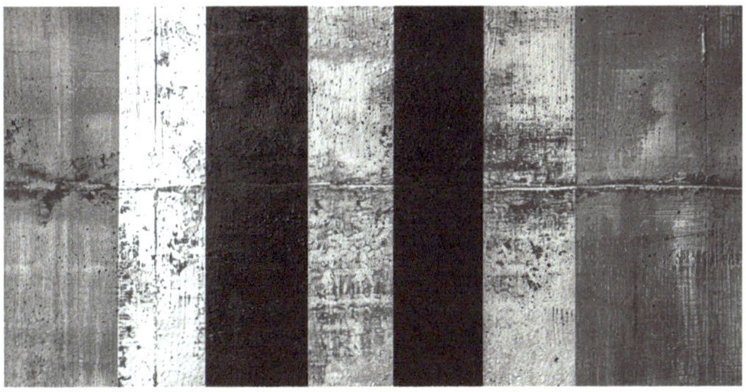

C

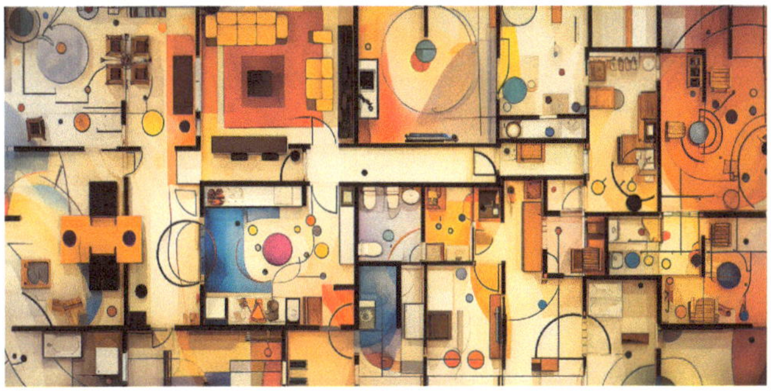

CHAPTER FIVE
MASTERING THE ART OF NETWORKING

Mastering the Art of Networking

From attending industry events to learning how to expand their professional network and uncover hidden job opportunities, graphic designers must attend industry conferences, workshops, and meetups to meet professionals and learn about various career paths. Find a mentor in the industry who can provide guidance, advice, and insights into different roles and environments. A practical consideration is to decide whether you are open to relocating or if you prefer to stay in a specific area.

Insights into networking techniques tailored to the graphic design industry:

Attend Design Events and Conferences: Attend design events, conferences, and workshops both locally and nationally to connect with fellow designers, industry professionals, and potential employers. These events provide valuable networking opportunities and keep you updated on the latest trends and innovations in the field.

Join Design Associations and Organizations: Join design associations and professional organizations such as AIGA (American Institute of Graphic Arts) or the Graphic Artists Guild. These organizations offer networking events, workshops, and resources specifically tailored to graphic designers, providing opportunities to connect with peers and industry leaders.

Participate in Online Design Communities: Join online design communities and forums such as Behance, Dribbble, or LinkedIn groups dedicated to graphic design. Engage with other members, share your work, and participate in discussions to expand your network and visibility within the design community.

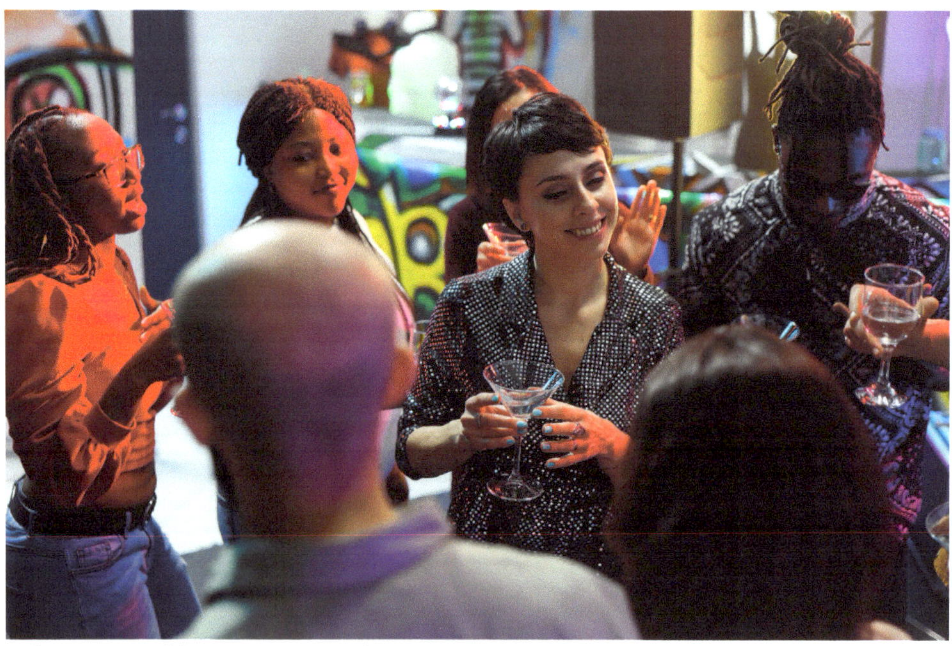

A diverse group of designers at a networking event

Utilize Social Media: Leverage social media platforms such as LinkedIn, Instagram, and X (formerly known as Twitter) to showcase your work, connect with other designers, and network with potential employers. Follow design-related hashtags, participate in design challenges, and engage with industry influencers to increase your visibility and establish connections.

Attend Portfolio Reviews and Critiques: Participate in portfolio reviews and critiques organized by design schools, agencies, or industry events. These events provide valuable feedback on your work and opportunities to connect with experienced professionals who may offer mentorship or job leads.

Reach Out to Alumni Networks: Connect with alumni from your design school or program through alumni networks, social media, or professional platforms like LinkedIn. Alumni can provide valuable insights, advice, and job referrals based on their own experiences in the industry.

Offer Pro Bono Work or Volunteer: Offer your design services pro bono or volunteer for nonprofit organizations, community events, or local initiatives. Not only does this give you an opportunity to give back to your community, but it also allows you to showcase your skills, expand your portfolio, and build relationships with potential clients or collaborators.

Attend Portfolio Nights and Design Expos: Attend portfolio nights, design expos, and student showcases hosted by design schools or industry organizations. These events often attract recruiters, creative directors, and hiring managers seeking new talent, providing opportunities to network and explore job opportunities.

Reach Out for Informational Interviews: Conduct informational interviews with professionals working in roles or companies you admire. Reach out via email or LinkedIn to request a brief meeting or phone call to learn more about their career path, industry insights, and potential job opportunities.

Follow Up and Nurture Relationships: After making connections, be sure to follow up and nurture relationships with your network. Send thank-you notes after meetings or events, stay in touch periodically via email or social media, and offer assistance or support when needed. Building and maintaining relationships is key to successful networking in the graphic design industry.

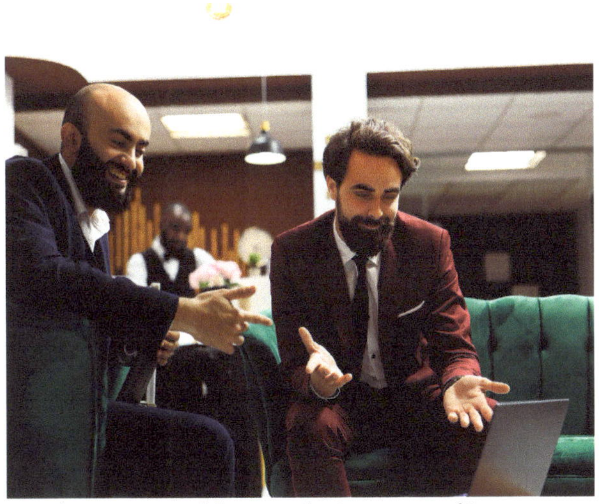

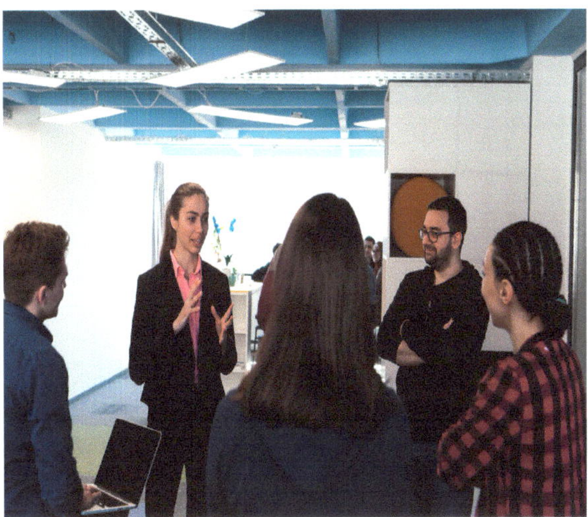

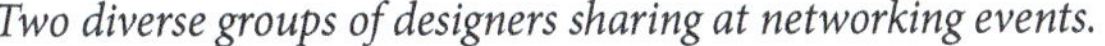

Two diverse groups of designers sharing at networking events.

CHAPTER SIX
TRANSITIONING FROM STUDENT PROJECTS

Transitioning From Student Projects

Transitioning from student projects to real-world client projects is a significant milestone for graphic design graduates. While it brings about challenges, it also holds potential for growth and development. Recent graduates can effectively navigate this transition and establish a successful career in graphic design.

Here are some key aspects that highlight the challenges and opportunities in this transition:

1. Client Expectations and Deadlines

Challenge: In the real world, designers must meet client expectations and adhere to strict deadlines. Unlike student projects where timelines may be more flexible, professional projects often have non-negotiable deadlines.

Opportunity: Learning to manage time effectively and understanding client needs helps build a professional work ethic and improve project management skills.

2. Complexity and Scope of Projects

Challenge: Real-world projects are often more complex and involve multiple stakeholders. Graduates may face tasks that are far more intricate than those encountered during their studies.

Opportunity: This complexity provides a chance to grow and develop a more sophisticated design approach. Working on diverse projects enhances problem-solving abilities and adaptability.

3. Technical Skills and Tools

Challenge: The industry may require proficiency in advanced software and tools that were not extensively covered during your education. Keeping up with the latest technology is crucial.

Opportunity: Continuous learning and up-skilling through workshops, online courses, and tutorials can bridge this gap. Gaining expertise in industry-standard tools enhances employability.

4. Feedback and Criticism

Challenge: Unlike academic settings where feedback might be more nurturing, real-world feedback can be direct and critical. This can be a shock to new graduates.

Opportunity: Constructive criticism from clients and colleagues is invaluable for professional growth. Learning to handle and incorporate feedback improves design quality and client satisfaction.

5. Professional Networking

Challenge: Building a professional network from scratch can be challenging for new graduates who may lack industry connections.

Opportunity: Engaging in networking events, joining professional organizations, and connecting with industry professionals on platforms like LinkedIn can open doors to job opportunities and collaborations.

6. Business Acumen

Challenge: Graduates often lack knowledge in areas like pricing, contracts, and client negotiations. Local Small Business Development Centers (SBDC) often offer classes, some online, on how to start a business, how to market yourself, etc. These are usually located at universities across the country and are sponsored by the Small Business Administration. Search for a SBDC located near you.

Opportunity: Learning about the business side of design through mentorship, online resources, and courses can provide a strong foundation for running a successful design practice.

Easing the Transition

Seek Internships and Entry-Level Positions

Gaining real-world experience through internships or entry-level positions is crucial for recent graduates. These opportunities provide practical insights into the day-to-day operations of design firms and agencies. Internships allow you to apply the theoretical knowledge acquired in school to real-world projects, thereby improving your practical skills. Entry-level positions also expose you to industry standards and expectations, helping you understand client interactions, project timelines, and the iterative nature of design work. Moreover, internships and entry-level roles often lead to permanent positions and build a professional network that can be beneficial throughout your career.

Create a Strong Portfolio

A strong portfolio is essential for job applications and career advancement. It should showcase a diverse range of skills, including typography, branding, web design, and more. Incorporating real-world projects, whether through internships, freelance work, or collaborations, demonstrates your ability to handle professional tasks. A well-curated portfolio not only highlights your technical skills but also your problem-solving abilities and creativity. Including detailed case studies for each project can provide potential employers with insights into your design process, from concept development to final execution. This comprehensive approach can make you stand out in a competitive job market.

Mentorship and Continued Education

Mentorship from experienced professionals can provide valuable guidance and insights that are not typically covered in academic settings. Mentors can offer advice on navigating the industry, improving your skills, and achieving career goals. Additionally, continuing education is vital to staying current with the latest design trends, software updates, and industry practices. Participating in workshops, attending design conferences, and enrolling in online courses can help bridge the gap between academic knowledge and professional expectations. This commitment to lifelong learning ensures that you remain adaptable and competitive in the ever-evolving field of graphic design.

CHAPTER SEVEN
EFFECTIVE CLIENT COMMUNICATION

Effective Client Communication

Effectively communicating with clients and understanding their needs and expectations is essential for building strong relationships, delivering successful projects, and ensuring client satisfaction.

By implementing the strategies below, you can enhance your communication with clients, meet their needs, and foster a positive working relationship:

1. Initial Communication

Understand Client Needs: Begin by conducting a detailed discovery session to grasp the client's needs, goals, target audience, and expectations. You may also consider using questionnaires or brief forms, if necessary.

Set Clear Expectations: Clearly outline your services, process, timelines, deliverables, and pricing. Make sure the client understands what to expect at each stage.

2. Establishing Communication Channels

Preferred Methods: Inquire about the client's preferred communication methods (email, phone, video calls, messaging apps) and establish regular check-in schedules.

Consistent Updates: Provide regular updates on the project's progress, even if it is just a confirmation that everything is on track. This helps build trust and keeps the client informed.

3. Documentation and Contracts

Written Agreements: Always have a written contract that includes project scope, deadlines, payment terms, and revision policies.

Project Proposals: Create detailed project proposals outlining the scope of work, milestones, timelines, and costs. Obtain the client's approval before commencing the project.

4. Active Listening and Feedback

Listen Actively: Pay close attention to the client's input, ask clarifying questions, and reiterate their points to ensure understanding.

Seek Feedback: Regularly ask for feedback at various stages of the project to ensure alignment with the client's vision and expectations.

5. Managing Revisions and Scope Creep

Clear Revision Policies: Define the number of included revisions and charge for additional changes. This prevents excessive revisions and scope creep.

Scope Control: If the client requests changes that affect the project scope, discuss the impact on timelines and costs before proceeding.

6. Professionalism and Responsiveness

Timely Responses: Respond to client communications promptly, ideally within 24 hours.

Professional Tone: Maintain a professional and friendly tone in all communications, demonstrating respect and appreciation for the client's business.

7. Tools and Platforms

Project Management Tools: Utilize tools such as Trello, Asana, or Basecamp to manage tasks, deadlines, and communications. Share access with clients for transparency.

File Sharing: Employ platforms like Google Drive, Dropbox, or WeTransfer for easy and organized file sharing.

8. Effective Meetings

Agendas: Have a clear agenda for each meeting to stay focused and productive.

Meeting Notes: Take notes during meetings and share them with the client afterwards to ensure everyone is on the same page.

9. Problem-Solving and Adaptability

Proactive Solutions: In the event of issues, present potential solutions rather than merely highlighting problems.

Professional Tone: Maintain a professional and friendly tone in all communications, demonstrating respect and appreciation at all times.

10. Post-Project Follow-Up

Client Feedback: After completing a project, it's important to ask for detailed feedback on your performance and the final product.

Long-Term Relationship: Stay connected with clients to create future opportunities and build lasting relationships.

Compensation - Clients and Freelance Designers

Charging clients as a freelance graphic designer requires a strategic approach to ensure you are fairly compensated while maintaining client satisfaction.

Here are steps and tips for effectively handling this process:

1. Determine Your Rate

Research Market Rates: Look into what other freelance graphic designers charge in your area and for similar services. Websites like Upwork, Fiverr, Glassdoor, and industry-specific forums can provide insights.

Calculate Your Costs: Consider your living expenses, business costs (software, hardware, taxes), and desired profit margin. Use this information to establish a minimum hourly rate.

Set Your Rate: Decide between charging hourly, per project, or on a retainer basis. Each method has its pros and cons.

2. Choose a Pricing Model

Hourly Rate: This is common for short-term projects or ongoing work where the scope is unclear.

Project-Based: This is best for well-defined projects. It helps clients understand the total costs upfront.

Retainer: This is ideal for long-term clients who need regular work. It provides a steady income.

3. Create Detailed Proposals

Scope of Work: Clearly define what the project includes (deliverables, number of revisions, deadlines).

Breakdown of Costs: Itemize your pricing, so clients understand what they're paying for.

Payment Terms: Specify the payment schedule (e.g., fifty percent upfront, fifty percent on completion), accepted payment methods, and late fee policies.

4. Contracts and Agreements

Written Contracts: Always use a contract to formalize the agreement. Include project scope, deadlines, payment terms, and intellectual property rights.

Clarity and Detail: Ensure everything is spelled out clearly to avoid misunderstandings.

5. Invoicing

Professional Invoices: Use invoicing software or templates to create professional invoices. Include your contact details, invoice number, date, itemized charges, payment terms, and due date.

Timely Invoicing: Send invoices promptly as per the agreed schedule. Typically, invoices are sent upon project milestones or completion.

6. Handling Payments

Upfront Payments: For new clients or large projects, request a deposit (usually 30-50 percent) before starting work.

Milestone Payments: For long-term projects, break the payment into milestones tied to project phases.

Payment Methods: Offer various payment options (bank transfer, PayPal, credit card) to make it convenient for clients.

7. Managing Revisions and Scope Creep

Revision Policy: Clearly define the number of revisions included in your fee. Charge for additional revisions beyond this.

Scope Changes: Any changes to the initial scope should be documented and agreed upon with adjusted pricing if necessary.

8. Communicate Value

Highlight Benefits: Emphasize the value and benefits your design work brings to the client's business, such as increased brand visibility, customer engagement, and sales.

Portfolio and Testimonials: Showcase your portfolio and client testimonials to demonstrate your expertise and the quality of your work.

9. Negotiation Skills

Be Flexible but Firm: Be open to negotiation but have a clear minimum rate you won't go below.

Value Over Price: Shift the conversation from just the cost to the value you provide.

10. Follow Up

Payment Reminders: Send polite reminders if payments are overdue.

Feedback and Testimonials: After project completion, ask for feedback and testimonials to use in your portfolio.

Example Script for Discussing Rates

Client: "What's your rate for designing a logo?"

You: "My standard rate for logo design is $500, which includes three initial concepts and two rounds of revisions. This ensures we can develop a logo that truly represents your brand. I can provide a detailed proposal if you'd like to proceed."

By following these steps and maintaining clear communication with your clients, you can effectively and professionally handle charging for your services as a freelance graphic designer.

Example of Designer and Client Communication Flow

- **Initial Email:**

"Hello [Client's Name],

Thank you for reaching out. I'm eager to learn more about your project. Could we schedule a call this week to discuss your needs and how I can assist you in achieving your goals?

I look forward to hearing from you.

Best regards,
[Your Name]"

- **Post-Meeting Summary:**

"Hello [Client's Name],

Thank you for the productive meeting today. Here's a summary of what we discussed:

Project Goals: [List out the goals]

Deliverables: [List out the deliverables]

Timeline: [List out the milestones]

Next Steps: [List out the next steps]

Please review and let me know if there are any adjustments or additions.

Best regards,
[Your Name]"

- **Progress Update:**

"Hello [Client's Name],

I wanted to provide you with a quick update on the project. We have completed [specific milestone/task], and everything is on track for our next deliverable, due on [date]. Please find attached the latest drafts for your review. (include visuals of mood boards, wireframes, sketches, prototypes).

I am looking forward to receiving your feedback.

Best regards,
[Your Name]"

Handling Client Feedback

Handling both positive and negative feedback from a client effectively is crucial for maintaining a strong professional relationship and ensuring project success. Always thank the client for their feedback. It shows that you value their opinion and understand what they appreciate.

Here are some strategies for dealing with client feedback:

Handling Positive Feedback - Express Gratitude

Always thank the client for their positive feedback. Show appreciation for their acknowledgment of your work. If the client compliments specific aspects of your work, acknowledge those details. It shows that you value their opinion and understand what they appreciate.

Example Response:

Thank you so much for your kind words! I'm thrilled to hear that you're happy with the logo design, especially the color palette. It was a pleasure working on this project.

Handling Negative Feedback - Express Gratitude

Thank the client for bringing any concerns about the website layout to your attention. Inform them that you value their feedback and apologize for any inconvenience caused. Commmit to revising the design so that it better aligns with their brand guidelines and that you will provide a new draft by the end of the week.

Follow-up:

After implementing the changes, follow up with the client to ensure they are satisfied with the resolution. Seek further feedback by asking if there are any additional adjustments or improvements needed. This shows that you are genuinely interested in understanding their perspective.

Reflect and Improve

Learn from experience: Use negative feedback as an opportunity to improve your skills and processes. Reflect on what went wrong and how you can prevent similar issues in the future.

Adjust practices: Make necessary adjustments to your workflow or communication methods based on the feedback received. Document feedback by keeping a record of all feedback. This will help you track client preferences and areas for improvement. Encourage clients to provide feedback throughout the project, not just at the end. Regular check-ins can help identify and resolve issues early. Anticipate potential concerns by staying ahead in your communication and delivering drafts or updates promptly.

By effectively handling feedback, you demonstrate professionalism, build stronger client relationships, and continuously improve the quality of your work.

Time Management Techniques for Designers

Managing time and resources efficiently is crucial for real-world graphic design projects. It ensures that deadlines are met, budgets are adhered to, and clients are satisfied. To effectively manage time and resources in such projects, consistent planning, organization, and communication are essential. These factors are key to achieving efficient project management in graphic design, leading to successful outcomes and satisfied clients.

Here are some practical tips and guidance for managing time and resources effectively in graphic design projects:

1. Set Clear Goals and Priorities: Collaborate with the client to define clear project goals, objectives, and priorities upfront. Identify the most important tasks and deliverables that need to be completed within the given time frame, and allocate resources accordingly.

2. Create a Project Timeline: Develop a detailed project timeline or schedule that outlines key milestones, deadlines, and deliverables for each phase of the project. Break down the project into smaller tasks and allocate time estimates for each task to ensure that the project stays on track.

3. Use Project Management Tools: Utilize project management tools and software such as Asana, Trello, or Monday.com to organize tasks, track progress, and collaborate with team members or clients. These tools allow you to set deadlines, assign responsibilities, and monitor project status in real-time.

4. Allocate Resources Wisely: Determine the resources needed for the project, including human resources, equipment, software, and budget. Allocate resources wisely based on project requirements and constraints to ensure that you have the necessary tools and support to complete the project successfully.

5. Break Down Tasks into Manageable Chunks: Break down larger tasks or projects into smaller, manageable chunks to avoid feeling overwhelmed and improve productivity. Set achievable goals for each task or milestone and focus on completing one task at a time to maintain momentum.

6. Manage Client Expectations: Communicate clearly with clients about project timelines, milestones, and deliverables to effectively manage their expectations. Set realistic deadlines and provide regular updates on project progress to keep clients informed and engaged throughout the process.

7. Prioritize Time Management: Allocate specific blocks of time for different tasks and avoid multitasking whenever possible to prioritize time management. Use techniques such as the Pomodoro Technique or time blocking to structure your workday and maintain focus on high-priority tasks.

8. Limit Scope Creep: Be vigilant about scope creep and avoid unnecessary changes or additions to the project scope that could derail timelines or exceed budget constraints. Clearly define project scope and deliverables upfront, and communicate any proposed changes to the client for approval.

9. Regularly Review and Adjust: Regularly review project progress against the established timeline and budget to identify any potential issues or bottlenecks early on. Make adjustments as needed to address challenges, reallocate resources, or revise timelines to keep the project on track.

10. Learn from Each Project: After completing a project, take the time to reflect on what went well and areas for improvement. Identify lessons learned and apply them to future projects to refine your processes, optimize resource allocation, and improve overall efficiency.

Time Management Tools

Task Management Software

These tools help designers create to-do lists, set deadlines, and prioritize tasks. Some popular task management tools are:

Todoist: Allows users to create tasks, set due dates, and organize tasks into projects.
Microsoft To Do: Integrates with other Microsoft products, allowing for task organization, deadline setting, and reminders.
Remember The Milk: Offers task organization with due dates, tags, and smart lists to help manage daily tasks effectively.

Project Management Tools

These tools are designed to manage complex projects, often involving collaboration with teams. Some popular project management tools are:

Asana: Enables project tracking, task assignments, deadlines, and progress tracking. Great for collaboration and keeping track of project timelines.
Trello: Uses boards, lists, and cards to help manage projects and tasks. Visually oriented and user-friendly, ideal for creative projects.
Basecamp: Combines task management, file sharing, and communication tools in one platform, helping teams stay organized and on the same page.

Time Tracking Apps

These apps help designers monitor how much time they spend on different tasks and projects, which is crucial for billing clients and improving productivity. Some popular time tracking apps are:

Toggl: Simple time tracking tool that allows users to start and stop timers for different tasks and projects. Provides reports and insights into time usage.
Harvest: Offers time tracking, expense tracking, and invoicing features. Suitable for freelancers and teams who need to track billable hours.

Clockify: Free time tracking tool that includes features like time sheets, reporting, and project tracking.

Digital Calendars

Digital calendars help designers schedule their tasks, appointments, and deadlines efficiently. Some popular digital calendars are:

Google Calendar: Integrates with various tools and allows users to schedule events, set reminders, and share calendars with team members.
Apple Calendar: Synchronizes across Apple devices and allows users to manage appointments, deadlines, and tasks.
Outlook Calendar: Part of Microsoft Outlook and useful for scheduling and managing meetings, tasks, and deadlines.

Integrated Suites

These tools combine various aspects of task management, project management, and time tracking into one platform. Some popular integrated suites are:

Notion: Versatile tool that combines note-taking, task management, and database features. Allows designers to create personalized workflows.
ClickUp: Integrates task management, project management, time tracking, and more. Highly customizable and suitable for both individual and team use.
Monday.com: Comprehensive work operating system that offers project management, task tracking, time tracking, and collaboration tools.

Additional Tools

Some specialized tools cater to specific needs of graphic designers. Some popular additional tools are:

Milanote: Idea organization tool that's perfect for brainstorming and project planning with a visual approach.
Evernote: Note-taking app that helps designers keep track of ideas, inspirations, and project notes, which can be synced across devices.

These tools, individually or in combination, can significantly enhance the efficiency and productivity of graphic designers by providing structure and clarity to their workflow. Like all software management tools and plans, there are pros and cons. FREE and Personal plans may have limitations, with certain features not being available. Most plans support web, mobile, or desktop platforms, while others require an Internet connection. However, some plans do offer free trial periods. Certain features are exclusively offered with the Business plan.

Inviting Clients to Your Home Office

Whether or not to invite clients to your home office depends on your specific situation and the nature of your business. If you choose to do so, ensure your home office is professional and welcoming. However, consider alternatives like co-working spaces, coffee shops, or virtual meetings for a more flexible approach. Always prioritize creating a comfortable and professional experience for your clients.

Pros of Inviting Clients to Your Home Office:

- **Cost-Effective:** Saves money on renting a separate office space.
- **Convenient:** Easy access to all your work materials and equipment.
- **Personal Touch:** Creates a more personal and relaxed atmosphere.

Cons of Inviting Clients to Your Home Office:

- **Professionalism:** Depending on your setup, a home office might not convey the same level of professionalism as a dedicated office space.
- **Privacy:** It can be challenging to maintain privacy and separate personal life from professional life.
- Distractions: Home environments can have more distractions, which might not be ideal for client meetings.

Considerations:

Home Office Setup:

- Ensure your home office is tidy, well-organized, and free from distractions.
- Have a dedicated meeting space with comfortable seating and necessary equipment (e.g., a conference table, chairs, presentation tools).

Client Expectations:

- Understand your clients' expectations. Some may prefer a more formal setting, while others may appreciate the personal touch of a home office.

Type of Business:

- If your business requires showcasing physical products or creative work, a home office might be suitable.
- For more formal or corporate clients, a neutral or professional setting might be preferred.

Privacy and Security:

- Ensure that your home office space respects both your privacy and that of your clients. Keep sensitive information secure and separate from personal areas.

Alternatives to Meeting Clients at Home:

Co-Working Spaces:

• Rent a meeting room in a co-working space for a professional environment without a long-term commitment.
• Co-working spaces often offer amenities like conference rooms, high-speed internet, and refreshments.

Coffee Shops and Cafes:

• Meet clients at a quiet coffee shop or café. This can be a casual and convenient option, but ensure it's appropriate for the nature of the meeting.

Client's Office:

• If feasible, visit the client's office. This shows flexibility and interest in understanding their work environment.

Virtual Meetings:

• Use video conferencing tools like Zoom, Microsoft Teams, or Google Meet for virtual meetings. This is increasingly accepted and convenient, especially for remote clients.

Renting Meeting Rooms:

• Some business centers or hotels offer meeting rooms for short-term rentals, providing a professional setting for important meetings.

Preparing Your Home Office for Client Visits:

First Impressions:

• Ensure the entrance to your home and your office space are clean and welcoming.

Amenities:

• Provide basic amenities like water, coffee, and tea.

Professional Ambiance:

• Decorate your office with professional decor, adequate lighting, and comfortable seating.

Technology:

• Ensure all necessary technology (Wi-Fi, projector, computer) is set up and functioning properly.

Distractions:

• Minimize potential distractions, such as noise from other parts of the house or interruptions from family members and pets.

Essential and Recommended Home-Office Eqipment

A freelance graphic designer needs a range of equipment to ensure they can work efficiently and effectively from home. By investing in the right equipment, a freelance graphic designer can create a productive and efficient home office environment, enabling them to deliver high-quality work consistently.

Here's a comprehensive list of essential and recommended equipment:

Essential Equipment:

Powerful Computer with Software

Desktop or Laptop: A powerful computer with high-resolution monitors is essential for design work. Ensure you have the latest design software installed. For laptops, MacBook Pro or a high-end Windows laptop.

Specifications: Look for a multi-core processor, at least 16GB of RAM (32GB is preferable for handling large files), a dedicated graphics card, and ample storage (SSD with 1TB or more).

High-Resolution Monitor

Primary Monitor: A high-resolution monitor with accurate color representation is vital. Look for a 27-inch 4K monitor with IPS technology for better color accuracy and wide viewing angles.

Secondary Monitor: An additional monitor can improve productivity by providing more screen real estate for multitasking.

Graphics Tablet

Wacom Intuos Pro or Huion Kamvas: These are industry-standard tablets that provide precise control for drawing and design work.

Reliable Internet Connection

High-Speed Internet: A fast and stable Internet connection is essential for uploading and downloading large design files, conducting video calls, and collaborating online and for seamless communication with clients and access to online resources. Invest in a good quality webcam and microphone.

Ergonomic Office Setup

Desk and Chair: Invest in a high-quality, ergonomic chair and a spacious desk to ensure comfort during long working hours. Adjustable desks that allow for sitting and standing can improve posture and reduce fatigue.

Natural Light: Position your desk near a window to take advantage of natural light, which reduces eye strain and boosts mood. Use a good desk lamp with adjustable brightness to ensure adequate lighting for detailed design work, especially in the evening.

Keyboard and Mouse: Ergonomic options like a mechanical keyboard and an advanced mouse can enhance productivity and reduce strain.

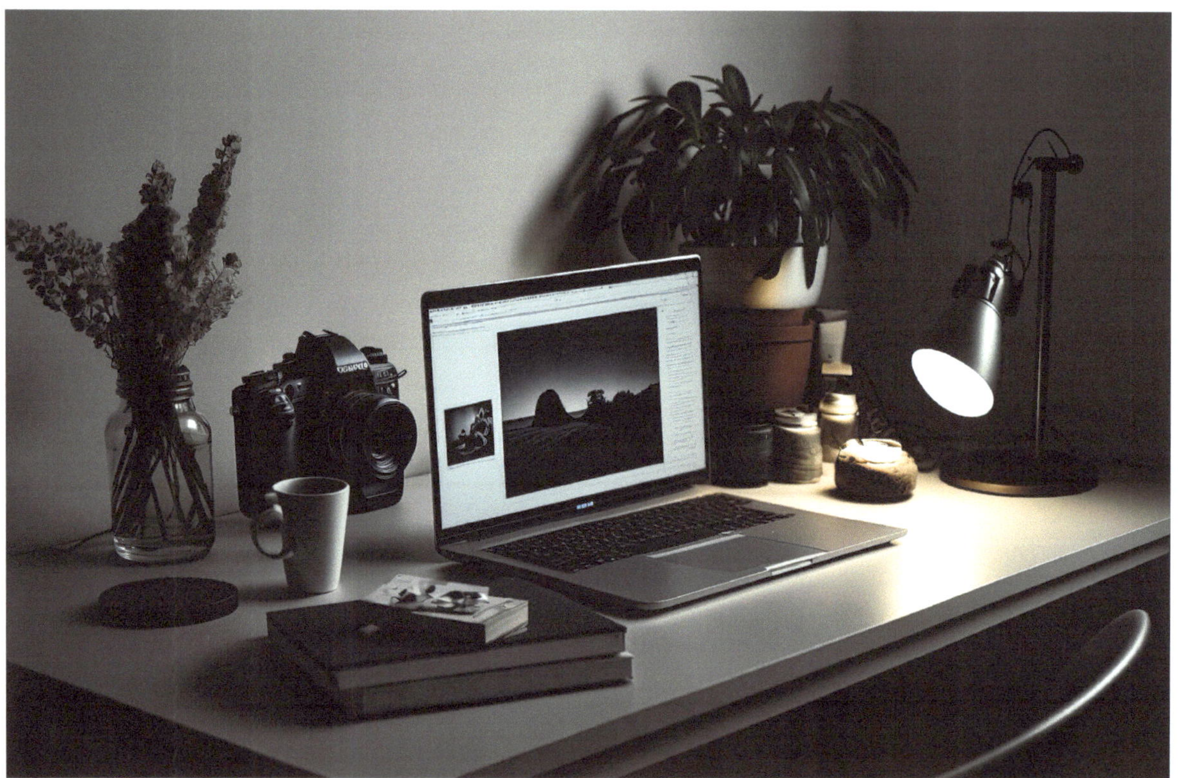

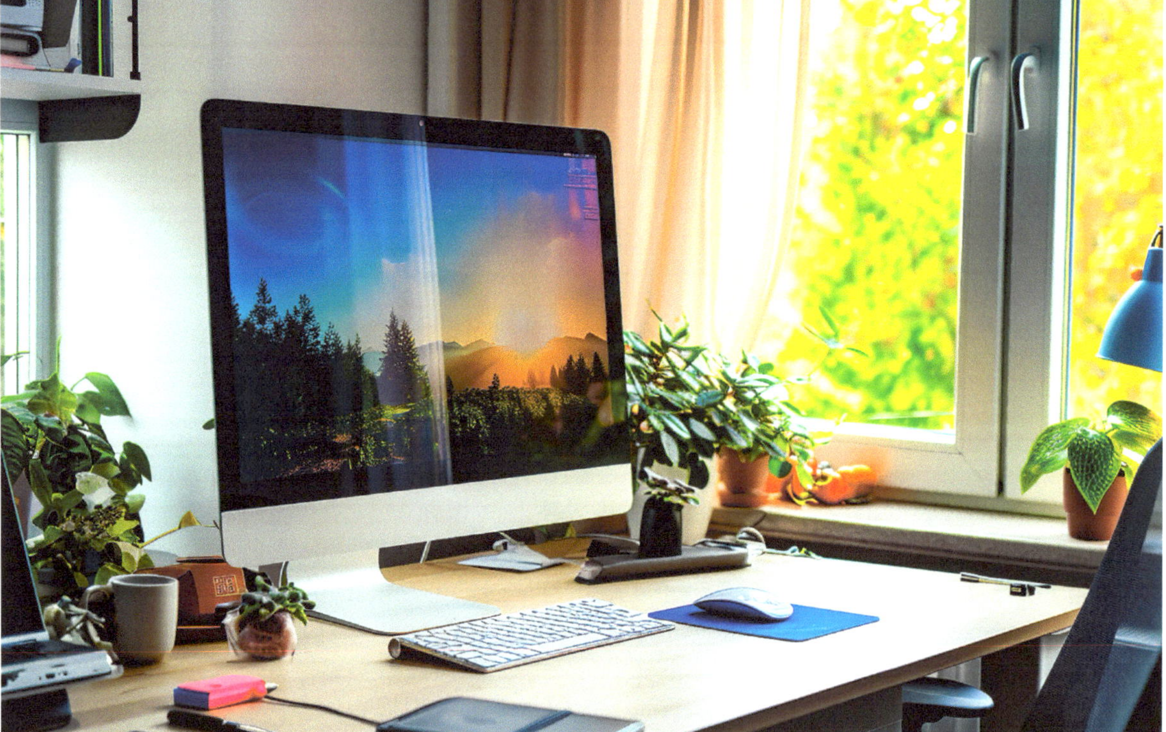

Freelancers workspaces at home showing laptop and desktop computers with adequate lighting (AI Generated).

External Backup and Storage for a Freelance Designer

External Hard Drives: High-capacity external SSDs or HDDs for backups and additional storage.

Cloud Storage: Services like Dropbox, Google Drive, or OneDrive for remote access and backup of important files.

Printer and Scanner

All-in-One Printer/Scanner: For printing proofs and scanning sketches or documents. Consider models like the Canon PIXMA or Epson EcoTank series.

Recommended Equipment:

Color Calibration Tools

Colorimeter: Tools like the Datacolor SpyderX Pro or X-Rite i1Display Pro to ensure your monitor displays colors accurately.

Camera and Photography Equipment

DSLR or Mirrorless Camera: For photographing your work or creating content. Options like the Canon EOS or Sony Alpha series are popular.

Lighting Kit: For consistent and professional lighting in your photos.

High-Quality Headphones or Speakers

Headphones: Noise-canceling headphones like the Bose QC35 or Sony WH-1000XM4 for focus and clear audio during video calls.

Speakers: High-quality speakers for accurate sound during multimedia work.

Mobile Devices

Tablet: An iPad Pro with Apple Pencil can be useful for on-the-go sketching and design work.

Smartphone: A high-end smartphone for quick communication, social media management, and on-the-go photo editing.

UPS (Uninterruptible Power Supply)

To protect your equipment and work from power outages.

Workspace Optimization:

Adequate Lighting

Natural Light: Ensure your workspace has good natural lighting.

Desk Lamp: An adjustable lamp with color temperature control.

Organization Tools

Desk Organizers: For keeping your workspace tidy.

Cable Management: Tools to manage and hide cables effectively.

Whiteboard or Cork board

For brainstorming, pinning inspiration, and keeping track of ideas.

Why is external backup and storage so essential?

All design agencies and corporations have backup systems, some more extensive than others. Freelance designers should too, as they heavily rely on their digital assets, such as client work, design files, software, and other resources. Losing these files due to hardware failure, accidental deletion, or other unforeseen events can have severe consequences. The worst day in any designer's life is when their hard drive "crashes" and they were not continuously backing up their work. It can be disastrous.

Here's why having external backup and storage solution is crucial for freelance designers:

1. Data Security and Redundancy

Protection Against Hardware Failure: Computers and hard drives are prone to failure. An external backup ensures that your work is safe even if your primary device malfunctions.

Redundancy: Having multiple copies of your work in different locations (e.g., external drives, cloud storage) reduces the risk of data loss. If one backup fails, you still have another copy.

2. Business Continuity

Minimized Downtime: In the event of data loss, having a backup allows you to quickly restore your files and resume work without significant delays. This continuity is vital for meeting deadlines and maintaining client relationships.

Client Trust: Clients trust you with their projects. Ensuring that their work is securely backed up demonstrates professionalism and reliability.

3. Organizational Efficiency

File Management: External storage helps in organizing and archiving projects efficiently. You can keep current projects on your primary device and move completed work to external storage, freeing up space and improving system performance.

Access and Retrieval: Properly backed up files can be easily retrieved whenever needed, reducing the time spent searching for old projects or client assets.

4. Data Protection and Compliance

Client Data Security: Freelancers often handle sensitive client data. Secure external storage solutions can help protect this data from breaches and unauthorized access.

Compliance: Depending on your location and the nature of your work, there might be legal requirements regarding data storage and protection. Regular backups can help ensure compliance with these regulations.

5. Peace of Mind

Reduced Stress: Knowing that your data is securely backed up provides peace of mind. You can focus on your creative work without worrying about potential data loss.

Risk Management: Effective backup solutions are part of risk management strategies, mitigating the impact of potential data loss on your business.

Implementing Backup Solutions

External Hard Drives: Invest in reliable external hard drives to store backups. Regularly update these backups to ensure they are current.

Cloud Storage: Services like Google Drive, Dropbox, and OneDrive offer secure cloud storage options. Cloud backups provide the added advantage of remote access and automatic syncing.

Backup Software: Use backup software to automate the backup process. Tools like Time Machine for Mac or Backup and Restore for Windows can schedule regular backups.

For freelance designers, external backup and storage solutions are essential to safeguard their work, ensure business continuity, and maintain client trust. By implementing robust backup strategies, designers can protect themselves from data loss, improve their workflow efficiency, and focus on delivering high-quality work to their clients.

Ensuring data security through external backups not only prevents potential disasters but also reinforces a professional image, essential for sustaining and growing a freelance design career.

CHAPTER EIGHT
CONTINUING PROFESSIONAL DEVELOPMENT

Continuing Professional Development

In the field of graphic design, it is crucial to engage in continuing education and professional growth. These practices enable you to remain current with industry trends, acquire new skills, and propel your career forward.

Here is an overview of various avenues for achieving these goals:

1. **Workshops and Seminars:** These short-term, hands-on learning experiences focus on specific topics or skills within graphic design. Led by industry experts or experienced designers, they offer interactive learning, skill-building, and networking opportunities.

2. **Online Courses and Tutorials:** Platforms like Udemy, Coursera, Skillshare, and LinkedIn Learning provide a wide range of online courses and tutorials. They cover topics such as software training, design principles, typography, branding, illustration, and web design. Online courses offer flexibility and convenience, allowing you to learn at your own pace from anywhere with an Internet connection.

3. **Conferences and Events:** Graphic design conferences and events bring together designers, educators, industry leaders, and enthusiasts. They offer networking, learning, and inspiration through keynote presentations, workshops, panel discussions, and exhibitions. Examples include Adobe MAX, AIGA Design Conference, and CreativePro Week.

4. **Mentorship Programs:** Aspiring designers can benefit from mentorship programs, where they learn from experienced professionals and receive personalized guidance and feedback on their work. Mentorship can take various forms, including one-on-one mentoring, group mentoring, or structured mentorship programs offered by design organizations, schools, or professional associations.

5. **Design Boot camps:** These intensive, immersive learning experiences are designed to accelerate your skills and prepare you for a career in graphic design. They cover a comprehensive curriculum, including design theory, software proficiency, portfolio development, and real-world projects. Design boot camps can be offered in-person or online and range in duration from a few weeks to several months.

6. **University and College Programs:** Universities, colleges, and art schools offer degree programs, certificates, and continuing education courses in graphic design and related disciplines. These programs provide comprehensive education and training in design theory, technical skills, and professional practice. They often culminate in a portfolio presentation or capstone project.

7. Professional Development Workshops: These workshops are designed to help graphic designers enhance their skills, knowledge, and career prospects. They cover topics such as portfolio development, client management, freelancing, entrepreneurship, and business skills tailored to the needs of designers in today's competitive market.

8. Self-Directed Learning: This involves independent study and exploration of design topics, techniques, and resources outside of formal education or structured programs. It includes reading books and articles, watching tutorial videos, participating in online forums and communities, and experimenting with new tools and technologies.

9. Industry Certifications like Adobe Certified Associate (ACA) or Adobe Certified Expert (ACE) validate proficiency in specific Adobe software applications commonly used in graphic design, like Adobe Photoshop, Illustrator, and InDesign. Achieving these certifications can enhance credibility and marketability as a graphic designer.

10. Specialized Courses and Masterclasses: These focus on niche areas or specialized skills within graphic design, such as motion graphics, UX/UI design, packaging design, typography, or digital illustration. They offer in-depth exploration of specific topics and techniques and are often taught by experts or practitioners in the field.

By exploring these avenues for continuing education in graphic design, you can expand knowledge, hone skills, and stay competitive in the dynamic field. Whether you prefer hands-on workshops, online courses, mentorship programs, or self-directed learning, there are plenty of opportunities available to help advance your career and achieve professional goals as a graphic designer.

Setting Career Goals for Advancement

To achieve success and fulfillment in your graphic design career, it is crucial to set career goals and create a plan for professional growth and advancement. By actively pursuing your career goals, you can create a plan for professional growth and advancement that aligns with your aspirations. Regularly review and reassess your goals, seek feedback, and stay proactive in taking steps towards achieving your career objectives.

Here are some strategies to help you set meaningful career goals and develop a plan for your professional development:

1. Reflect on Your Values and Interests: Begin by reflecting on your values, interests, passions, and long-term aspirations as a graphic designer. Consider what motivates you, what you enjoy most about your work, and what you hope to achieve in your career. Your career goals should align with your values and personal aspirations.

2. Identify Your Strengths and Areas for Improvement: Assess your strengths, skills, and areas for improvement as a graphic designer. Identify your unique talents, technical skills, and areas where you excel, as well as areas where you may need to develop or enhance your skills. This self-assessment will help you identify areas of focus for your professional growth plan.

3. Set SMART Goals: Set SMART (Specific, Measurable, Achievable, Relevant, Time-bound) goals that are clear, actionable, and achievable within a specific time frame. Break down your long-term career goals into smaller, manageable milestones and objectives that you can work towards incrementally.

4. Establish Short-Term and Long-Term Goals: Define both short-term and long-term career goals that align with your overarching vision for your graphic design career. Short-term goals may include acquiring new skills, completing a certification, or expanding your portfolio, while long-term goals may involve career advancement, entrepreneurship, or industry recognition.

5. Research Career Paths and Opportunities: Research different career paths, roles, and opportunities within the graphic design industry to identify potential avenues for growth and advancement. Explore job openings, industry trends, and emerging areas of specialization to inform your career goals and development plan.

6. Invest in Continuing Education and Skill Development: Invest in continuing education, training, and skill development to enhance your expertise and stay current with industry trends and technologies. Take advantage of workshops, online courses, conferences, and mentorship programs to acquire new skills and knowledge relevant to your career goals.

7. Build Your Professional Network: Build and nurture your professional network within the graphic design industry by connecting with peers, mentors, industry professionals, and potential collaborators. Networking provides valuable opportunities for learning, collaboration, and career advancement, as well as access to job opportunities and resources.

8. Seek Feedback and Mentorship: Seek feedback from colleagues, mentors, and industry professionals to gain insights into your performance, strengths, and areas for growth. Actively seek mentorship from experienced designers or leaders in your field who can provide guidance, support, and advice on navigating your career path.

9. Create a Development Plan: Develop a formal development plan that outlines your career goals, objectives, and action steps for achieving them. Include specific strategies, timelines, and milestones for acquiring new skills, gaining experience, and advancing your career. Regularly review and update your development plan to track your progress and adjust your goals as needed.

10. Stay Flexible and Adapt to Change: Stay flexible and open to new opportunities, challenges, and changes in the industry. Be willing to pivot, take calculated risks, and explore new directions in your career path as you gain experience and evolve as a graphic designer. Embrace lifelong learning and continuous improvement to remain adaptable and resilient in the face of change.

By implementing these strategies and actively pursuing your career goals, you can create a plan for professional growth and advancement that aligns with your aspirations and helps you achieve success as a graphic designer. Regularly review and reassess your goals, seek feedback, and stay proactive in taking steps towards achieving your career objectives.

Staying Inspired and Motivated

Staying inspired and motivated as a graphic designer while maintaining a healthy work-life balance is essential for your overall well-being and creativity. You can stay inspired, motivated, and balanced while pursuing your creative passions and professional aspirations. Remember to prioritize your well-being, nurture your creativity, and cultivate a fulfilling and sustainable career in graphic design.

Here are some pieces of advice to help you stay inspired, motivated, and balanced in your graphic design career:

1. Set Boundaries: Establish clear boundaries between work and personal life to prevent burnout and maintain a healthy balance. Set specific work hours, take regular breaks, and prioritize self-care activities such as exercise, hobbies, and spending time with loved ones outside of work.

2. Find Your Creative Outlet: Explore creative outlets outside of graphic design to recharge and inspire your creativity. Engage in activities such as painting, photography, writing, or music that allow you to express yourself creatively and explore new ideas and perspectives.

3. Seek Inspiration Everywhere: Stay curious and open-minded by seeking inspiration from diverse sources and experiences. Explore art, architecture, nature, travel, literature, and other forms of creative expression to spark new ideas and ignite your imagination.

4. Stay Connected with the Design Community: Stay connected with the design community by attending events, workshops, and conferences, and networking with fellow designers and creatives. Surround yourself with like-minded individuals who share your passion for design and can offer support, encouragement, and inspiration.

5. Set Meaningful Goals: Set meaningful goals and objectives for your design career that align with your values, interests, and aspirations. Whether it's mastering a new skill, completing a personal project, or achieving a career milestone, having clear goals can help keep you focused, motivated, and engaged in your work.

6. Embrace Continuous Learning: Embrace a mindset of continuous learning and growth by seeking out opportunities to expand your knowledge, skills, and expertise in graphic design. Take advantage of workshops, courses, tutorials, and mentorship programs to enhance your abilities and stay current with industry trends and technologies.

7. Experiment and Take Risks: Don't be afraid to experiment with new ideas, techniques, and approaches in your design work. Take calculated risks, push your creative boundaries, and challenge yourself to step outside of your comfort zone to discover new possibilities and grow as a designer.

8. Celebrate Your Achievements: Celebrate your achievements, both big and small, to acknowledge your progress and boost your confidence and motivation. Take pride in your work, reflect on your successes, and recognize the impact of your contributions to your clients, colleagues, and the design community.

9. Practice Mindfulness and Self-Care: Practice mindfulness and self-care to reduce stress, increase resilience, and enhance your overall well-being. Incorporate mindfulness techniques such as meditation, deep breathing, or yoga into your daily routine to cultivate a sense of calm and balance amidst the demands of your work.

10. Listen to Your Inner Voice: Listen to your inner voice and trust your instincts when it comes to your creative process and decision-making. Tune into your intuition, passions, and instincts to guide you in pursuing projects and opportunities that align with your values and bring you joy and fulfillment as a graphic designer.

By incorporating these pieces of advice into your daily life and career as a graphic designer, you can stay inspired, motivated, and balanced while pursuing your creative passions and professional aspirations. Remember to prioritize your well-being, nurture your creativity, and cultivate a fulfilling and sustainable career in graphic design.

CHAPTER NINE
MAKING A LASTING IMPACT

Making a Lasting Impact

To make a lasting impact in your job and advance your career, there are several strategies you can adopt that will demonstrate your value to the organization and position you for growth.

Here are some key steps to help you stand out and progress in your career:

1. Exceed Expectations

Deliver high-quality work: Consistently produce excellent work by paying attention to details, striving for accuracy and creativity.

Meet and beat deadlines: Show reliability by completing tasks ahead of schedule whenever possible.

2. Continuous Learning and Skill Development

Stay updated: Keep yourself informed about industry trends and new technologies by reading industry publications, taking online courses, or attending workshops.

Certifications and education: Pursue relevant certifications and advanced degrees that will enhance your skill set and credentials.

3. Take Initiative

Identify and solve problems: Look for areas in your department or organization that need improvement and propose appropriate solutions.

Volunteer for new projects: Demonstrate your willingness to take on additional responsibilities by volunteering for new and challenging projects.

4. Build Strong Relationships

Networking: Cultivate a strong professional network both within and outside your organization. Attend industry events, join professional groups, and engage with colleagues on social platforms like LinkedIn.

Mentorship: Seek out mentors who can provide guidance and support for your career growth. Additionally, mentor junior colleagues to demonstrate leadership and a willingness to give back.

5. Communicate Effectively

Clarity and conciseness: Ensure that your communication, whether in writing or speaking, is clear, concise, and impactful.

Active listening: Show respect and attentiveness in meetings and discussions by actively listening and engaging with your colleagues.

6. Showcase Your Achievements

Document successes: Keep a record of your accomplishments and the impact of your work. Use metrics and concrete results to demonstrate your contributions.

Self-promotion: Learn to tactfully promote your successes. Share your achievements with your manager during performance reviews and updates.

7. Develop Leadership Skills

Lead by example: Demonstrate professionalism, integrity, and a strong work ethic.

Team collaboration: Foster a collaborative environment and work well within teams, showing that you can lead and contribute effectively.

8. Be Adaptable

Embrace change: Be open to change and adaptable to new circumstances. This flexibility can make you a valuable asset during times of transition.

Innovative thinking: Propose and implement innovative ideas that can drive efficiency and success within your role or the organization.

9. Seek Feedback and Act on It

Request feedback: Regularly seek feedback from peers and supervisors to identify areas for improvement.

Implement suggestions: Act on constructive criticism to improve your performance and demonstrate a commitment to personal and professional growth.

10. Set and Pursue Career Goals

Define goals: Clearly define your short-term and long-term career goals.

Create a plan: Develop a strategic plan with actionable steps to achieve your goals. Regularly review and adjust your plan as needed.

CHAPTER TEN
CHANGING CAREERS & MOVING ON

Changing Careers and Moving On

The ideal time to change careers and establish new goals can vary for each person and depends on different factors.

However, certain signs and situations may indicate that it's a suitable time to make a change:

1. Dissatisfaction with your current job: If you consistently feel unhappy, unfulfilled, or stressed in your current role, it may be time to consider a new career path. Long-term job dissatisfaction can have a negative impact on your mental health and overall well-being.

2. Lack of career progression: If you find that there are limited opportunities for growth, advancement, or skill development in your current career, it might be time to explore other paths that offer better prospects.

3. Changing interests and passions: Over time, your interests and passions may change. If you discover a new passion that aligns more closely with your personal values and aspirations, it might be worth pursuing a career change.

4. Market changes and industry decline: If your current industry is experiencing a decline or significant changes that threaten job stability, it may be wise to transition to a more stable and growing field.

5. Financial stability: Having a financial cushion can make the transition smoother. If you have savings or other financial support, it can be an ideal time to take the risk of changing careers.

6. Opportunities for education and training: When opportunities for further education, training, or certification in a new field arise, it can be an opportune time to pivot your career. This can equip you with the necessary skills and knowledge for a successful transition.

7. Supportive network: Having a supportive network of family, friends, or professional mentors can provide the encouragement and guidance needed for a career change. If you have such a network, it can be a good time to take the leap.

8. Personal life changes: Life events such as relocation, family changes, or achieving significant milestones can also prompt a reassessment of career goals. These moments can provide a natural point to consider new directions.

Steps for setting new goals:

1. Self-assessment: Reflect on your skills, interests, values, and what you want to achieve in your career. Write them down.

2. Long-Term Goals: Envision where you see yourself in five to ten years. Write it down.

3. Research: Investigate potential career paths and industries that align with your assessment. Look into job prospects, required skills, and industry trends.

4. Networking: Connect with professionals in the field you're interested in. Attend industry events, join relevant groups, and seek informational interviews.

5. Skill development: Identify gaps in your skills and seek opportunities for training or education to fill those gaps. Write them down.

6. Create a plan: Develop a step-by-step plan with achievable milestones to guide your transition. Write them down.

7. Stay flexible: Be open to adjustments and remain adaptable as you navigate your new career path.

DEFINITIONS OF SOME TERMS WITH EXAMPLES

Target Audience

Definition: The specific group of people for whom a product, service, or piece of content is intended. This group is often defined by various demographics, behaviors, interests, and needs.

Example: *For a children's book, the target audience would be children aged 5-8 and their parents.*

Visual Narrative

Definition: The use of images, graphics, and visual elements to tell a story or convey a message. It integrates visual components to create a cohesive and compelling storyline.

Example: *A comic strip or a storyboard used in filmmaking.*

Wireframes

Definition: Simplified, skeletal representations of a website or application layout, focusing on the arrangement of elements and functionality rather than design details. Wireframes are used in the early stages of design to plan the structure and user flow.

Example: *A black-and-white outline of a webpage showing the placement of the header, footer, navigation menu, and content sections.*

Prototype

Definition: An early, interactive model of a product that demonstrates its functionality and design. Prototypes are used to test concepts, gather feedback, and refine the final product before development.

Example: *A clickable version of a mobile app that allows users to navigate through the app's features.*

Mockup

Definition: A high-fidelity static representation of a design that shows what the final product will look like. Mockups include detailed visual elements, such as colors, typography, and images, but are not interactive.

Example: *A full-color image of a website homepage, displaying the final design without interactive elements.*

Optimize

Definition: The process of making something as effective, efficient, or functional as possible. In design and development, optimization often involves improving performance, speed, and user experience.

Example: *Compressing images on a website to reduce load times and improve performance.*

Responsive

Definition: A design approach that ensures a website or application adjusts and performs well on various devices and screen sizes, providing an optimal user experience across desktops, tablets, and smartphones.

Example: *A webpage that rearranges its layout and resizes images when viewed on a mobile device.*

Renders

Definition: The process of generating a final visual output from a model or design. In digital design and 3D graphics, rendering creates realistic images or animations from 3D models, incorporating lighting, texture, and shading.

Example: *A high-resolution image of a 3D architectural model showing detailed textures and lighting effects.*

By understanding these terms, designers can effectively communicate their ideas and processes, leading to more successful and collaborative projects.

Summary

Transitioning from student to professional involves essential steps like updating your portfolio, choosing its style, color, and design, presenting 3D work, identifying your target audience, and refining your resume and cover letter. Customizing job application materials for specific postings and setting yourself apart from the competition is crucial; tailoring your applications to stand out will increase your chances of landing interviews. Preparing for job interviews requires understanding common questions, developing your own questions, and navigating different interview types, including video interviews, with an emphasis on presenting your best work and negotiating pay.

Finding employment opportunities aligned with your skills and career goals involves understanding the job market and comparing nonprofit versus for-profit design work. This includes exploring various career paths such as roles in advertising agencies, design studios, corporate settings, and freelance work. Networking is vital in the graphic design industry, requiring techniques like attending industry events, expanding your professional network, uncovering hidden job opportunities, utilizing social media, connecting with alumni, and nurturing relationships for career growth.

Moving beyond the structured environment of academia to tackle real-world design briefs and client expectations requires strategies for managing time, being open to feedback, and developing business acumen. Effectively communicating with clients involves understanding their needs and expectations, documenting work, creating contracts, and negotiating compensation. Setting up a home office and ensuring proper external storage and backup are also essential.

Continuing education and professional growth are crucial for setting career goals and staying inspired. This involves engaging in ongoing learning and seeking advancement opportunities in the field of graphic design. Making a lasting impact in your job and advancing your career requires demonstrating your value to the organization and positioning yourself for growth. Recognizing the ideal time to change careers and establishing new goals is important, especially when signs indicate it's time for a change. This involves identifying the right moment to transition and making a smooth shift to new career opportunities.

It is the author's hope that graduating seniors of graphic design, and instructors and educators of graphic design will find this book a useful companion resource guide for students in their graphic design courses.

About the Authors

McCulloch

An award-winning graduate of Ringling School of Art and Design in Sarasota, Florida, Linda McCulloch has lived and worked in Atlanta for 40+ years. After several years in the graphic design, advertising and printing industries, she founded Design That Works Communications Inc., a company rooted in helping businesses find creative solutions that really work for their marketing needs.

She has been described by copywriting colleagues as "the only literate art director/graphic designer in Atlanta," due to her exceptional editing, proofreading, and copywriting skills. She believes that accurate syntax, grammar, and correct usage of language in any marketing communication effort are just as important as excellent design and execution.

Over the years she has served not just as creative director, graphic designer and illustrator to her numerous clients, but has also written and edited many of their marketing communications. She has also guest lectured at several institutions of higher learning and led workshops on effective branding, marketing, and communications.

Maugé-Lewis

The author, an alumna of Howard University (Washington, DC), now a Professor Emerita at Kennesaw State University (KSU) in Georgia, has played a key role in developing and coordinating the Graphic Communication concentration in the School of Art and Design at KSU for over two decades. With her expertise and innovative approach, she has not only won awards for her design work but has also presented at numerous national and international conferences. In recognition of her contributions, she was featured as one of twelve "Educators to Watch" by Graphic Design USA (GDUSA) in 2018. GDUSA, a renowned organization providing news and information to graphic designers and the broader creative community since 1963, continues to recognize her achievements.

Maugé-Lewis has received the Distinguished Teaching Award in the College of the Arts at KSU twice. Under her guidance, her students have achieved remarkable success, winning awards at local, national, and international levels, including GDUSA, the Society of Publication Designers, and the "48 Hour Re-Pack" competitions among others. Many of her students now flourish as Art Directors, Brand Managers, Web Designers and Marketing specialists in the graphic design field – while some are carving out amazing careers at companies such as Disney, Facebook, and Apple, among others, with a few starting their own design businesses.

Maugé-Lewis is committed to teaching, designing and writing on graphic design. This is her second title in a series of three books on graphic design.

www.ingramcontent.com/pod-product-compliance
Ingram Content Group UK Ltd.
Pitfield, Milton Keynes, MK11 3LW, UK
UKHW060119300726
14090UKWH00002B/273
* 9 7 9 8 9 9 0 4 1 4 1 2 9 *